Creative Cost-Benefits Reinvention

Creative Cost-Benefits Reinvention

How to Reverse Commoditization Hell in the Age of Customer Capitalism

Christian Dussart

palgrave
macmillan

CREATIVE COST-BENEFITS REINVENTION

First published in 2010 by
PALGRAVE MACMILLAN®
in the United States—a division of St. Martin's Press LLC,
175 Fifth Avenue, New York, NY 10010.

Where this book is distributed in the UK, Europe and the rest of the world, this is by Palgrave Macmillan, a division of Macmillan Publishers Limited, registered in England, company number 785998, of Houndmills, Basingstoke, Hampshire RG21 6XS.

Palgrave Macmillan is the global academic imprint of the above companies and has companies and representatives throughout the world.

ISBN: 978–0–230–10530–0

Library of Congress Cataloging-in-Publication Data

Dussart, Christian.
Creative cost-benefits reinvention : how to reverse commoditization hell in the age of customer capitalism / Christian Dussart.
p. cm.
ISBN 978–0–230–10530–0
1. Marketing. 2. Product differentiation. 3. Value. 4. Consumer behavior. 5. Cost effectiveness. I. Title.

HF5415.D878 2010
658.15′52—dc22 2010017337

A catalogue record of the book is available from the British Library.

Design by Newgen Imaging Systems (P) Ltd., Chennai, India.

First edition: November 2010

10 9 8 7 6 5 4 3 2 1

Printed in the United States of America.

To my wife for her patience and support.

To my (expanding) family and close friends.

CONTENTS

FIGURES

FOREWORD

Perhaps no other topic is more fundamentally important to marketing than differentiation. Differentiating products and services is how consumers are given choices and how companies build their brands. Differentiation creates marketplace variety and interest. A well-differentiated product or service can increase consumer satisfaction and the prices customers are willing to pay. Price premiums improve company profitability and allow companies to invest in growth.

So in theory, differentiation can improve the fortunes of consumers and companies alike. But unfortunately, theory does not always match practice, and many companies fail to enjoy the benefits of differentiation for one simple reason: their products or services are just not seen by consumers as meaningfully different or better than other products or services. A hypercompetitive, ultratransparent modern world puts the pressure on companies to continually innovate but to do so in a relevant manner, to create differentiation.

Failure to innovate and stay relevant can lead to erosion in differentiation and a painful descent into commoditization hell, where gains and losses are driven solely by costs and prices and there are no real winners. Commoditization is a painful game to play. The solution is clear: differentiation is key.

Some fresh and even radical thinking, however, is required to help guide these efforts. The basic themes are clear. Marketers must stay close to consumers and understand all the different ways they create value. In many ways, one of the best things that happened as a result of the very painful economic recession that began in the fall of 2008 was that marketers had to consider all the different ways they created value for customers. There was really no other way to sustain sales and nurture customer loyalty.

In recent years, smart marketers have recognized that it is a mistake to be overly focused on price reductions and discounts that could harm long-term brand equity and price integrity. Rather, smart marketers have focused on increasing—and clearly communicating—the value that their brands offered customers, making sure consumers fully appreciate *all* the different financial, logistical, and psychological benefits involved in their offerings as compared to the competition.

Taking a broad view of how to create customer value is an essential piece of the differentiation puzzle. But new ideas and stimulation are badly needed to tackle such a challenging and potentially intractable problem. With this book, Christian Dussart helps to fill that gap. He offers fresh perspectives and insight honed from years of careful observation and thought. He provides a thoroughly up-to-date view of the commoditization phenomenon and persuasively describes what companies should do about it. And his message concerning the central importance of customer value creation could not be more timely or compelling. To use what little high school French is still with me, it is more than ever the *raison d'être* of every organization.

Kevin Lane Keller
E. B. Osborn Professor of Marketing
Tuck School of Business at Dartmouth

PREFACE

> "Professor Einstein, Professor Einstein!
> The questions of this year's exam are the same as last year's!"
> "True," he replied, "but this year all the answers are different."
>
> —Anecdote from Albert Einstein's
> tenure as a professor at MIT

The purpose of a preface is to describe not only the genesis of the idea for the book but also how it developed, blossomed, and finally came to fruition.

It all began in the late 1990s at MIT's Sloan School of Management. I was teaching a marketing course in the Sloan Fellow Program, delivered over one year to a large group of business executives from all over the world, many of whom worked at General Motors (GM). Their presence in this program was justified for obvious historical reasons: the institution and program bore the name of the founder of GM, Alfred Sloan, who had the foresight to understand that value creation lay in presenting several lines of automobiles to meet the needs of several social classes. He also believed in offering cars in various colors. This was an astute way to stand out from the famous Ford Model T, available only in black. The Model T was already a type of commodity born from industrial mass production, portrayed by Charlie Chaplin in the movie *Modern Times*.

The Fellows from GM constantly showed me that they had probably already foreseen the difficulties their company would face by always almost casually asking the same question: Could you tell us exactly how to create value? Back then, I simply replied that they had to produce quality cars, which they themselves acknowledged they were not actually doing.

As they interacted with younger MBA students at Sloan, the GM staff ultimately admitted that their cars were fairly unattractive and not very "sexy," in their parlance, unlike the BMW!

Although the quality problem inherent in the three largest American auto manufacturers, GM, Ford, and Chrysler, was quite important (and should have been resolved), I also wondered what caused so many other products to lose their cachet so quickly. They plunged almost instantaneously from the specialty stage to the status of a commodity, prematurely falling into price markets with devastating effects on margins and hence on net profits.

My early works attempted to analyze why this happens. I concluded that, from among myriad new factors, the combined effects of market globalization and business digitization triggered a vast commoditization movement, with an immediate adverse effect on brands.

The role of brands in the decision-making processes of consumers and buyers has diminished significantly. Brands will not disappear, but they no longer serve as a systematic guarantee of premium pricing and even less of brand loyalty. The perceived parity among brands and the prevalence of comparison shopping changed everything.

I then began presenting my preliminary ideas to executives at seminars. My analysis and diagnoses were very well received. These are the same executives who criticized me in the early years of the twenty-first century for leaving them to fend for themselves. In fact, they were right. They accused me of erecting a massive wall—the wall of commoditization—and failing to propose any tools to help them scale it or get around it.

At that time, I had not yet found a way to reverse the trend and counter the negative effects of brand commoditization and the concomitant collapse of profit margins. My only excuse, or escape hatch, if you will, was to explain that I was simply presenting my current state of knowledge, the point I had reached in my reflection on the topic. I was not popularizing an existing theory. I was in the midst of a conceptual moment in time and was following my intellectual train of thought wherever it led me.

I then began to focus on creation of value within the fight against commoditization. I realized the existence of two things: (1) the morass (sadly, this word is not too strong) clouding the notion of value and (2) the difficulty of assembling my ideas in a coherent whole as my work environment (market economy, company life, technical evolutions, etc.) was erupting all around me.

After accepting that I could no longer control or consolidate all the new ideas that I perceived on a sustained and daily basis, I began to falter and became like the mathematician in the film *A Beautiful Mind*, who spent nights and days obsessively piecing together bits of information to form a coherent and homogeneous picture puzzle.

Enervated, I requested a sabbatical year, during which I invested all my energy into devising a set of measures that would create value, with value for the customer as the priority.

Honestly, I thought writing the outline would be much easier. I spent six whole months shoring up the outline of my book. To compound the situation, a few months after my sabbatical year began, the famous recession of November 2008 struck. I didn't know which way to turn—whether to try to follow the events as they happened, especially because they were directly related to my topic, or to ignore what was going on. Of course, I had to take the lessons from the recession into account and integrate them in my analysis. In the end, this severe recession and its negative effects on the behavior of some companies had very positive effects on my work, even if the knowledge gained came at a high price!

Wanting to test my preliminary solutions to the problem of creating value in companies, I began to aggressively confront companies where the leitmotif of top management was basically to trap clients.

I realized there were two types of companies: those that, in a state of panic, turn exclusively and frantically to cost cutting, sawing off the branch on which they are sitting, and those companies that continued to strive with all their might to create value for the customer by designing their costs rather than cutting them blindly. I then decided to focus exclusively on the second group of companies, which are certainly fewer but which deserve to be helped. I abandoned the others, believing I have no more time to waste with them, at least not in the near future.

My last epiphany concerned the crucial importance of social values in the company—that a balance must be struck between financial arrangements and quality to offer customers. People must come first.

The complete intellectual process described in this book ranges from analysis to strategic recommendations. The common thread throughout this approach is the obsession with customer satisfaction, the search for a fair balance between the long and short term, and the will to reinvent business models by harnessing innovation.

More than ever, I believe controlled evolution is superior to a brutal bloody revolution. I am also convinced that marketing quality drives customer satisfaction, spurs organic growth and market share, and ultimately delivers positive financial results.

I consider all of the company's functions equally important. However, business models must make creation of value for the customer a priority. This involves finding the best solution, even a commercial one, to customers' problems.

One thing is certain: if you start designing your business model based solely on costs, your efforts will be fruitless. However, if you carefully define the value proposition you will deliver to the customers and orchestrate your functions to achieve this by controlling costs, you are on the road to reasonable, well-deserved profits.

In his State of the Union speech in February 2010, President Obama rightly emphasized the need for people to stand up and take responsibility. He made it clear that long-term prosperity must prevail over short-term gains.

It is time to infuse the business world with decency!

Christian Dussart
July 2010

ACKNOWLEDGMENTS

I would like to thank two people in particular. Without their help, I don't know if I could have come this far.

The first is Michel Patry, director of HEC Montréal. He understood the scope of the project perfectly and how important it was to me. Because the task was so complex, he spontaneously advised me to take a sabbatical year, telling me in no uncertain terms that I needed it. Upon my return, once the book was published, we would find a way to share the benefits within our institution. It is rare to encounter such a positive and proactive individual. He met with me several times during the editing process, and his confidence in me was unwavering. I appreciate his support tremendously. His professional collaboration was indispensable. Thank you, Michel!

The second person is Karen Sherman, my linguist. She plunged into the subject with little prior knowledge of the intricacies of the field. She pushed me relentlessly, goading me to clarify some ideas or rewrite a paragraph that fell short, keeping everything clear and simple. She achieved a herculean task. We sometimes locked horns but always for just cause. I owe her a great deal. She is a true professional. More than just a translator and a linguist, she truly takes the project to heart. Without her, I could never have expressed my ideas so cogently and eloquently. Thank you, Karen!

Introduction: All You Need Is C(l)ash

> We admit it, we have disappointed you. At times, we violated your trust by letting our quality fall below industry standards and our designs become lackluster.
>
> —Excerpt from a letter GM sent to 29,000 employees in late 2008

The Three Monkeys: Hear No Evil, See No Evil, Speak No Evil

You have probably seen the famous image from Japan of three monkeys sitting side by side. They embody the principle "see no evil, hear no evil, speak no evil." The first monkey is covering his eyes, the second is covering his ears, and the third is covering his mouth. Sometimes there is a fourth one that symbolizes the principle "do no evil"; this one may be covering his abdomen or just crossing his arms.

These days, that image easily brings to mind the overhyped meeting in Washington in November 2008, in which the CEOs of the three big U.S. car manufacturers were begging for money. Not for small change but for a first official bailout of about $30 billion (at least)! A fourth claimant joined the chorus—the president of the United Auto Workers (UAW), making the analogy with the symbol nearly perfect.

One after another, they described their serious financial difficulties, their voices dripping with compassion as they expressed their deepest concerns for their companies, for the domestic auto industry, and for the entire economy. The GM CEO should have also mentioned China and Europe, where the company was also hitting the wall. They unhesitatingly attributed their catastrophic situation to the crisis alone. None of them pleaded guilty to any charges. They closed their "bail-out" speech by affirming that they had no further plans apart from production.

Obviously, they had all suffered from chronic marketing myopia for the last decade at least. They produced unattractive cars riddled with technical problems. As early as 2000, GM had officially acknowledged the poor quality of its products in a disastrous advertising campaign entitled "Sorry, we are very sorry." Almost incredibly, they told the general public, and their most loyal customers in particular, that although they were aware of systematic quality problems with their cars, they were not taking the issue very seriously! On top of that, for many years, they did not understand how to create added value for their customers. Did they even try? Predictably, both their market share and their profitability declined steadily. Nobody tried to brake against the downfall.

As for production, the only thing GM still excelled at, at least according to their own claims, was the accumulation of gas-guzzling cars like the emblematic Hummer. They also reinforced their lobbying with the federal government to minimize constraints related to pollution. They could then continue with business as usual. Worst of all, they did not abandon their costly zeal for power cars. During the January 2009 Detroit Auto Show, GM shamelessly flaunted a mega-machine: the 750-horsepower Chevy Camaro!

Taken together, these facts are very hard to swallow. Public anger is justifiably mounting, as is reluctance to dole out more money to companies. In countries such as Japan, this level of incompetence would probably have triggered spontaneous resignations among top executives, but not at GM. They are probably well aware of how lucky they are. It was only in late March 2008 that GM's CEO was forced to resign by President Obama himself. When you ask for such huge sums of cash, your bargaining position definitely becomes more precarious.

Since the beginning of the drastic downturn, the final, ugly consequences of irresponsible business attitudes and behaviors emerged simultaneously across many economic sectors, from banks and financial institutions to steel producers, farms, and even Original Equipment Manufacturers (OEMs), which developed a form of an "all you need is cash" attitude—officially called a "bailout." Candidates for a government bailout are multiplying around the world. One Russian candidate is the country's largest maker of hand-painted dolls. Even the major petroleum companies brazenly asked for grants! That is the last straw!

Risky business practices are on the rise, but at the same time, a worldwide purge of malpractice is under way.

Businesspeople are not the only ones to suffer from a total lack of foresight. Clearly, they have placed too much priority on shareholder value to the exclusion of other areas. They have moved from dilapidation to SOS. Yet economists, too, have been bewitched by market euphoria. Their forecasts of economic growth, the price of a barrel of oil, productivity, and many other economic indicators were invariably overly optimistic. Business analysts have amplified companies' "cheery" words. They repeatedly gave individual shareholders poor recommendations. Journalists lacked a critical stance, neglecting their role as a communication liaison between companies and their audiences. Consumers, meanwhile, were dazzled by easy money and easy credit. Consumption was portrayed as the key driver of economic development, without any restrictions. The balloon of overconsumption and financial manipulation was inflated to the bursting point. The collateral damage has been enormous. It was a very big balloon indeed!

Now the short-term goal is to frenetically reinflate the patched global economic balloon, to keep it airborne by all means, whatever the cost, without knowing where the turbulent winds of the deep recession will carry it or if and when the balloon will land. The skin of the balloon is being radically patched, and it is ready to burst again. Inflation plus subsidies create an explosive mix. Nobody knows what the fallout will be. The debate over grants is raging: Is this the right solution or not? On the demand side, the world is awash in goods, which means that it will take more than programs to spur spending to jump-start the economy.[1]

One thing is for sure: the abundant usage of bailouts is stoking even greater public anger because this money belongs to the taxpayers. Bailouts are widely perceived as the government pouring billions of dollars down a bottomless economic pit. Overall economic trust, a major driver of growth and stability, is quickly evaporating between customers and the business world, between business partners, and even worse, between banks. More and more people are calling for regulation and insisting that social and human ideals be placed at the heart of business practices. This may be very hard to implement, but it is absolutely necessary.

The lack of coherent, solid explanations about the downturn is pushing many so-called business experts and top executives into a reactive mode. They argue that this catastrophic situation was unpredictable—not true. In a powerful article published in March

2008, before the beginning of the crisis, the authors refute the common assumption that major external factors like economic downturns bring companies down most often.[2] In fact, executives may be surprised to discover that the biggest threat to continued corporate growth is executives' inability to make sound decisions about strategy and organizational change. I believe many executives are just trying to hide their inability to grasp and manage the "big company disease" that emerged about a decade ago, linked to the dual massive development of globalization and digitization. This disease is a sign of the rampant commoditization effect.

This sweeping global trend has driven the overall evolution of the economy and related business practices (including unsavory ones). It acts like the Gulf Stream in the "red" ocean of business activities, where hypercompetition leads to bloodiness.[3] The financial crisis, or more specifically the total loss of control over decadent yet institutionalized financial manipulation, has been the spark that ignited the huge economic explosion. A cynical observer would say that the financial crisis is the straw that broke the camel's back!

The Core Arguments

The Central Idea: Focus on Commoditization First; Downturn Will Follow

The financial crisis and its painful social consequences are just the tip of the iceberg. Below the surface of the water is an all-encompassing economic phenomenon: the ongoing commoditization process. Despite today's scourges (escalating poverty, lack of purchasing power, job crises, and homelessness, for example), companies should not be distracted by the profusion of short-term remedies to the downturn. Many opportunists are touting, or seeking, overhyped, fast-selling, profitable business tricks. The proliferation of buzzwords—such as Quantitaive Easing (QE), Boomeconomics, Diworsification, Gazump, and so on—is a symptom of a shotgun approach to economic recovery. Companies should let the dust settle and then focus on reversing the tide of commoditization. They need to make the creation of customer value their top priority. They must learn how to navigate through the chaos and its extreme outcome, the current downturn. Keep in mind that the downturn will ease off, even if it takes several years. Commoditization, on the other hand, is here to stay. Economic crises build and decline in a never-ending cycle. This is why in the long term the market outperforms the company.[4]

Such a radical statement—that commoditization is the main cause of business change—certainly requires an explanation. The concept of commoditization will now be introduced. It will be explored in detail in the first chapter.

If you have the unpleasant perception that your business organization is just one of many players in your industrial sector, with identical offers and results, join the club! You are operating in what is currently called survival or reactive mode, a professional context that is definitely undesirable. Your customers perceive that the only thing differentiating your offer from that of your competitors is the price. They might be totally wrong—your organization may have unique business characteristics. But because perception might as well be reality, this problem is particularly frustrating. The bad news is that you are suffering from commoditization, which some top executives refer to as "big company disease."[5] This disease is not limited to big companies, and even worse, there is no cure. The good news is that you can escape commoditization if you cultivate differentiation throughout your organization, which means you develop real and perceived uniqueness in the way you perform, uniqueness that, most importantly, is hard for competitors to replicate. This transformation demands a lot of time and effort. It is anxiety provoking, too, because you have to shed many traditional patterns related to the way you conduct your business. Staying in survival mode, however, is a nightmare. The choice is yours! If you have already decided that differentiating your entire organization is a poor investment because customer decisions will always be about price, I hope this book will convince you otherwise. But if you are actively looking for leads and a roadmap to escape this dead end, then this book is for you!

Two basic assumptions should drive your willingness to escape the commodity trap. The first one is as follows: "Strategic differentiation of your business model consistently brings higher returns than making cost-cutting process improvements or adding product features that competitors can readily match."[6] The second one is this: "Marketing is the science and art of differentiation."[7] Indeed, it is, but this differentiation must span the entire organization.

Addressing both statements, and without downplaying necessary cost-cutting activities, this book focuses first on marketing strategies (as opposed to marketing tactics) that increase perceived customer value, the only type of value that ultimately matters. It goes beyond the traditional, entrenched boundaries of marketing, such as product or brand differentiation, and extends to unique and possibly disruptive business dimensions that can generate, directly or indirectly, added and perceived value for customers. This is called a strong customer value proposition or CVP. I am not delivering this message as a marketing expert (or professor) but rather as a business analyst who adopts both a marketing and global perspective. This change in perspective is very significant because it positions marketing as a key strategic approach to value creation, a cornerstone of a holistic business model.[8]

If you are ready to face this challenge, keep reading to learn how to reverse the tide of commoditization. To avoid being defeated by difficulties related to commoditization, always keep in mind that reactive people are losers and proactive people are winners. Actions speak louder than words.

The Central Question: How to Escape from Commodity Hell

The central question is how can you break out of commodity hell? How do you escape the gravitational pull of the commodity trap? How do you ride out the storm? The scope of the challenge is staggering because of the extreme complexity of the problem. Solutions cannot be found in traditional mass-marketing principles and practices alone. Obviously, new ways of creating value are required. The core notion of "value" must be clearly defined in the minds of executives, a prerequisite that unfortunately is not always met. Past experience speaks for itself. When we refer to value, are we speaking of value for the shareholders, the employees, or the customers? This is the heart of the perpetual debate between the short- and the long-term.

New business attitudes are also needed. Above all, commoditization should not be perceived solely as a business threat but also as an opportunity. A SWOT (Strengths, Weaknesses, Opportunities, Threats) analysis of commoditization can help companies adjust their business models to these dramatic economic realities. An impartial vision is absolutely necessary. Here again, objectivity is not always a given: people much prefer success stories to failures, even if recovering from failures is invariably more productive than resting on one's laurels. Resistance to change is hard to dispel. Some businesspeople are becoming exasperated because they feel bombarded by "new business models." Most likely, they can no longer cope with the pace of change and they feel like they are drowning in disruptions. This might be because the economy is changing at a much faster pace than any individual company has been able to match without losing control.[9]

Finally, appropriate sets of strategic responses should be developed to help businesspeople skirt the commodity trap. They should not be limited to cost management, a practice that is, regrettably, too commonplace. In companies, the resilience regimen should be a long-term fitness plan, not a crash diet.[10] In addition, value-oriented marketing strategies ought to be put in place. These strategies should focus on creating a relationship with customers that involves revamping traditional brand equity approaches by banking more than ever on brand personality to create authenticity. For example, one of the key attributes of a brand is called the perceptual distance, that is to say the perception among the customers that the brand really cares for them, in every which way. If you want to create relationships with your customers, your brand must be perceived by the customers as close and connected to them. It is about cultivating relationships ahead of building brands.[11] Companies must also learn how to manage customer equity effectively. It is not a question of replacing brand equity with customer equity. Balancing incremental and disruptive marketing approaches is the real challenge. Managing a radical yet smooth marketing evolution and avoiding an unpredictable revolution is the best game plan. The goal is to foster customer engagement, the only way to reverse the tide of commoditization. There is room for improvement here. In short, making a balanced shift from brand equity to customer equity its main strategic focus is the best way for a company to preserve and boost its business equity. Here is a dirty little secret, though: most executives can't articulate their business strategy in a simple statement. Of course, if they cannot, then nobody else can, especially during a crisis.[12]

Marketing should not be considered the only pivotal function in a company. It should be viewed as a major support (among many others) for customer value creation. This enlarged and inclusive perspective underlies the specific approach of this book, as outlined in the first paragraph of this general introduction. The intellectual framework of reference is defined by the overall convergence of marketing and IT in a global world. Welcome to the new competitive reality!

The Central Idea: Believe and Invest in a Solid CVP

In general, the more turbulent the economy, the more difficult it is to implement and promote a real orientation toward customers. In a severe downturn, operating conditions as a whole deteriorate. Focusing on customer needs and satisfaction becomes extremely difficult and even risky. Some executives have stopped listening. Customers simply do not meet their short-term needs. They are fixated on plugging holes, trying to keep their business ship afloat and consequently save their jobs. This is quite understandable, even if it makes the work of an outside advisor much harder, as I can attest. What is really hard to understand (and to accept) is that many executives have been devastated by the finance world, yet they still rely devoutly on finance to get them out of this mess. It's quite paradoxical, even masochistic. At any rate, human psychology definitely comes into play in these circumstances.

Conversely, the handful of companies weathering the downturn have made their customers a priority. In fact, the necessary focus is as clear cut for them as it is hard to sell to the others. Sadly, hurt executives are immune to customer-oriented arguments!

There is only one certainty in uncertain times: if you do not make your customers a priority, you will not survive, never mind thrive. Normal operating procedures are passé. Breakthrough management ideas should be developed for a world in which the game has been changed irrevocably. For example, the open-source initiative, which appeared in the first decade of the twenty-first century with the free software movement, could expand to other business activities and translate into crowdsourcing activities to improve innovation in development of products or services, advertising, or communication copy strategies. More specifically, the Google model could help Detroit: adopting the search giant's open-source model could strengthen the connection of the Big Three of American car manufacturing to car buyers.[13] Admittedly, the idea of using Google's business approach to facilitate GM's recovery is, at first glance, farfetched. But it just might work.

Financial tools actually deter businesses from breaking new ground: they act as innovation killers throughout an organization, especially when it comes to revamping or reinventing business models.[14] Instead of pitting finance and marketing against each other in a frenetic battle, businesses need to promote the full integration of all the functions of an organization around a solid customer proposition that acts as the hub of its mission statement. Building a sustainable company is critical.[15]

Frenetic cost cutters who reject all alternatives are sawing the branch they are sitting on. They are honing the art of creative self-destruction instead of the harmful destruction of creativity. They are making a dire situation even worse. Sadly, such an irresponsible reaction is fairly common. It afflicts the business world even more often during a recession.

That is why this book presents a highly constructive approach, aimed at reversing the tide. It requires both courage and tenacity. But it can be done, and it is a good way to weed out bad top executives. The emphasis is on "cost designing" as opposed to "cost cutting." Instead of "profits," I advocate "building profitability." This is not a matter of semantics. The main goal is to show that success lies in the artful juxtaposition of diverse business components. These components can be compared with the parts of a musical score that must be taken up in an order to create real music; similarly, among the business components, CVP comes first, followed by an integrated set of functions and an adequate cost design, with the goal of building fair profitability.[16]

The Trade-offs: Can We Do It? Yes We Can!

The basic concept of commodity is broad. It has generated abundant theories and related publications in areas as diverse as economics, social science, and political science. Marx himself delved into this subject, evidently from a more political angle. There has been a fierce debate over the difference between "commodification" and "commoditization." This book does not add to it, but I clarify both the perspective and approach.

The history of commoditization and its economic waves is not discussed here, nor are the commoditization of business processes per se or the impact of commoditization on employees and society in general. Although very important, these topics are not germane to this book.[17] The analysis of individuals will be restricted to new behaviors and attitudes regarding consumption or buying behaviors, depending on whether we are referring to B2C (business-to-consumer) or B2B (business-to-business), because even commodities have customers.[18] The expected changes in attitudes within a renewed leadership profile will also be outlined.

Granted, using an explanatory model to illustrate that globalization and digitization are the two main drivers of commoditization is a necessary simplification of a complex worldwide reality. Although globalization is portrayed as the main driver of deflation, deflation might also be sparked by digitization and the resulting bargaining power of consumers and industrial buyers. To capture the complexity and close interrelations between economic variables, I simplify the picture. However, it is important to be realistic and open to other perspectives. Presenting a model as a figure where every box is connected by lines of causality largely results in an incomprehensible jumble nobody fully understands. Worse, such a model might be completely disconnected from reality.

The main difficulty is consequently to integrate many of the latest, admittedly disparate business ideas, incremental or disruptive theories, principles, and business models to create a more meaningful overall picture, showing only the major connections between them and helping businesspeople better understand what is going on today in the global markets, which will help them anticipate the future. A turbulent economic and an obscure business reality are given meaning. Without a clear grasp of the economic forces at play, companies cannot make sound business decisions. A thorough analysis is needed, but the intellectual process should go further: knowing why you are hitting the wall might ultimately be constructive if you know how to avoid repeating the same mistakes.

The chapters that follow cut though the hype and zero in on how the combined effects of globalization and digitization are transforming the marketing, branding, sales, and after-sales functions in industries. I have deliberately avoided buzzwords.

Most importantly, I have tried to be open-minded and avoid being mired in old, entrenched theoretical visions. Too many of the publications directly or indirectly related to our subject are strictly oriented toward the revitalization of mature markets. For example, most of the studies of emergent consumers—Chinese, Indian, and Brazilian—adopt an "exotic" perspective. They describe the ongoing development of these people's consumption behaviors, with the implicit underlying assumption that the end state of their learning process will be consumption similar to that of the so-called developed countries or incumbents. Are we the perfect model to follow? Are they really going to follow in our footsteps? Their cultural differences are so vast that we should expect to see distinct patterns of consumption in many areas. A global, dual perspective is definitely more appropriate, one that focuses on the proper development of a global market portfolio in which balanced and adapted marketing strategies between emergent and declining markets are considered. Consequently, impartial, global views of customer value creation take precedence over scrutiny of particular aspects of the phenomena.

The Intellectual Process

This book flatly rejects the myth of commoditization as a fatality and endorses a proactive business reaction to commoditization as a key to survival. Freezing in a reactive manner by calling for protectionism or nationalism, and doing nothing are not viable options. Hoping commoditization will fade away is not a feasible strategy either. Fatalism guarantees you will be trapped. Facing this new economic reality demands both business vitality and courage. It is above all a question of personal attitude as an executive, a proactive attitude toward commoditization itself, and a more enlightened attitude toward value creation. Your "good" or "bad" attitudes toward commoditization and value creation will determine whether you are in or out of the game. It's that simple!

To help you form a proactive attitude, the design of this book progresses from theory to action, from meaningful analysis to pertinent strategic recommendations. Businesspeople need more than just a description of a turbulent reality: they are eager for business leads and roadmaps. Honestly, they deserve them, as long as those recommendations are not depicted as business tricks or snap formulas.

The objective of Part 1 is to help readers fully understand how commoditization works, where it comes from, and what its main business impacts are. An in-depth analysis is necessary. If one does not clearly understand the problem, there is no way to find effective solutions.

Part 2 defines the business prerequisites for action. The issue of commoditization is controversial and might easily trigger nonconstructive emotional reactions. To avoid this pitfall and to exhibit intellectual integrity, I present and strongly defend my position on some basic business perspectives. A neutral approach is both unrealistic and inappropriate here. The starting points must be clear to the readers. These ideas are not universally embraced, which is part of the problem. The definition of value and what it stands for will be addressed. As for business responses to both commoditization and the downturn, the debate over ideals and business models will be clarified. In addition, the components of successful business models and their internal organization will be discussed. The starting point is a solid CVP.

The third step (Part 3) concerns action: how to constructively reverse the tide of commoditization. You can either struggle against it or benefit from it, depending on the configuration of your business situation (products, services, and markets). For example, in India, some entrepreneurs are surfing the wave of commoditization: their cost structure is extremely low and they deliver quality. The initial choice is yours, but the final outcome and business outputs are not! First, a set of new business logics is integrated in a framework for action. At the core of the model is the CVP-driven business reinvention logic. Around it, three other logics radiate from the hub to form the spokes of a wheel: the first logic is about effectuation, related to development of the business model, from an entrepreneurial perspective; the second logic is the service-dominant marketing approach, in which marketing is a crucial support but is no longer considered the pivotal function of any company; the third logic is that of fair profitability resulting from a value-for-money perspective. After defining the integration of these new business logics, I have highlighted the creation of attractive CVPs—specifically, the way executives can create customer value. A long list of customer value-oriented marketing strategies is then presented. These strategies are categorized according to their degree of disruption, from incremental to disruptive to extreme.

The fourth and last step, addressed in the conclusion, directly challenges the negative position of some top executives and, to a certain extent, malpractice: the systematic and impulsive rejection of interest in customer satisfaction as the "ultimate question."[19] New managerial precepts are then required at the corporate level. New organizational structures, incentives, and relationships must also be put in place. Scenario planning is needed here, along with a close look at the radar screen. What's more, the new realities require new leaders. Today's successful leaders bear no resemblance to the leaders who ruled business life 20 years ago. Because of the very nature of the current economic situation (combining high value and low price), executives must begin by mapping their price-quality competitive position. Lastly, marketing should be repositioned as a strategy to fully benefit the entire organization's development and even ensure its survival. In a nutshell, reinventing business models from a strong marketing perspective is the intellectual leitmotif of this book. It is not limited to industries, business models, or managerial practices: it also concerns human resources, especially marketing experts or leaders with a real customer-oriented vision.

Detailed Presentation of Contents

Here is a brief overview of what can be found in each chapter and section.

Part 1: ABCs of Commoditization

Chapter 1 sets the stage. It starts with a description of the new economic reality. This reality is fueling the chaotic economy, described as a world of collisions. The combined effects of these collisions foster the emergence of commoditization. Commoditization is then defined, followed by an introduction to the commodity trap. On the supply side, the focus is on the impacts of globalization. As long as the world is "flat" (Yes, it is!),[20] it can be considered the frontage of a large shop window: brand proliferation appears nearly unlimited.[21] On the demand side, the impact of digitization is being felt. Customer empowerment is clearly the dominant trend. We have moved into a global mass market of one. Consumers are becoming "prosumers." Comparison shopping is an increasingly frequent buying behavior, while networking, peering, (that is, P2P or Peer-to-Peer) and sharing are new economic realities businesspeople must contend with, whether they like it or not. Two major combined effects of globalization and digitization are emerging: very-low-cost business models and the collective intelligence perspective applied to business.

Chapter 2 explores the combined impact of the two dominant effects from a market-oriented perspective. New buying behaviors and attitudes are emerging worldwide. The mass market is vanishing. Purchasing power is becoming a major concern, especially when it is shrinking. Luxury for the masses is taking off. The famous price-quality relation is seriously being reconsidered. Manufacturer brands and distributor brands are playing musical chairs to win customers' dollars. What's more, the Internet has become the largest store in the world. Other mobile devices will likely get on board pretty soon.

Part 2: Defining Business Prerequisites (and Ideals) Prior to Action

Chapter 3 presents a real value-for-money business perspective, namely the search for a balance between creating customer value and cost designing. The extreme concept of broad-based cost cutting as a sole remedy for a difficult business situation is rejected. Business models that combine innovation in product policy, logistics, and customer experience will generate the biggest bang for the buck, driving both growth and stock value.[22] Execution must flow from clear positioning—nothing more, nothing less. Finally, efficiency-driven execution that emphasizes collaboration and synergies is endorsed.

Chapter 4 discusses reinventing business models as a response to commoditization. Despite the polemic on the superiority of ideals over new business models, reinventing business models should be the main strategic response to the downturn. Ideals and business model conception are inseparable: it is a chicken-and-egg problem. Knowing all the elements of a business model is necessary to assemble the final collage. The CVP is central to this collage. It is the cornerstone of the entire argument in this book. Of course, sustaining an existing business model, even one that has proven successful, does not mean freezing it!

Part 3: Reversing the Tide of Commoditization Constructively

Chapter 5 introduces the pitfalls to avoid when one is trying to break out of commodity hell. A multifunctional approach to CVP-driven reinvention of models is endorsed. Companies must stop trying to apply old solutions to cope with new realities. Bending obsolete paradigms and management tools out of shape is hardly a workable solution. The real and practical meaning of customer-centric innovation is explained. New business logics are integrated in a process that serves as a basic framework for action.

Chapter 6 presents ways executives can create value for their customers, using the framework developed in the previous chapter and with customer-value proposition (CVP) as the corner stone. First of all, a list of key business issues is submitted and practical responses are provided for each of them. Following this, the recommended business approaches to customer-value creation are listed based on degree of innovation, ranging from incremental only to very disruptive (what I call the disruption spectrum). The prevalent perspective consistently focuses on the customer or buyer side depending on whether the business environment is B2C or B2B. So, all these approaches (or recommendations) are evaluated according to their capacity to propose solutions to customers' personal or professional problems.

Conclusions

It is not surprising that this extreme marketing turbulence, so extensive in range and magnitude, requires dramatically new settings, from revised frames to new internal cultures, not to mention specific recommendations related to their implementation and execution. The conclusion reviews only the requirements considered major—that is, those strictly related to customer value creation—by looking at business models from a marketing perspective.

First, the extremely negative and irresponsible leitmotif some top executives are promoting within their organization, which boils down to "F – – – the customer!" is strongly criticized. If you notice this type of approach in a company, walk away and work for more positive people. The situation is hopeless. You must be selective and avoid businesspeople with this attitude.

Second, do not give up the fight to make customer satisfaction the ultimate index of performance, vis-à-vis your customers (and within your business). Your performance on this index will not be limited to marketing activities. It will have a significant impact, either positive or negative, on your financial performance within an average time frame of one year. The relationship is not hypothetical. If you fail to deliver value to your customers, do not be surprised if your company is forced to ask for a bailout (in the best case), to file bankruptcy, or to do both before too long.

Third, long-term commoditization and the increasing severity of the series of crises strongly underline the need for new organizational structures, new cultures, new incentives, and new relationships. The ideal profile of leadership needs to be thoroughly reenvisioned.

Fourth, given the prevalence of the price-quality relationship, which is typical of the birth of low-cost and high-value business models, systematically mapping your price-quality competitive position should be one of your top priorities. Because no marketing research is needed for this inexpensive exercise, it can (and should) be done by all companies.

Fifth, repositioning of marketing as strategy[23] and championing this repositioning within the company[24] are two simultaneous business requirements. The marketing function should be a top business consideration and not be limited to the four Ps (where the P's stand for Product, Publicity, Place [=Distribution], and Price). Yes, rethinking marketing is necessary.

To summarize, the reinvention of your entire industry and your business models, within both a marketing strategy and a renewed cost perspective, is the key to survival. Commoditization changes everything except the central rule of business: profitability. It is making the building of profitability even more complex. Focusing on one side exclusively, be it marketing or costs, will inevitably lead to failure. Simultaneous appropriate management of both sides is crucial. Silos (or closed functions) are obsolete. The company is today a collage of equal functions and all these functions should be integrated around the customer value proposition. Customer value creation must come first!

PART 1

ABCs of Commoditization

CHAPTER 1

The Tide of Commoditization

In the long run, everything is a toaster.
—Bruce Greenwald, professor, Columbia Business School

Greenwald's statement is clever, glib, and memorable, Michael Schrage comments.[1] But is it true? Some manufacturers are still making good money selling toasters and better toast. Commoditization isn't inescapable, but companies need a specific strategic focus to prevent it from becoming a black hole. Many once-mighty companies now find themselves fighting for their survival in "Me-Too Hell" as fakes and copies are easier when you are dealing with basic commodities, such as toasters; therafter, it is harder to differentiate one brand from another.

The situation can be stated as follows: the enemy—commoditization, without a doubt; the victim—every company that fails to lead in innovation; the penalty—plunging growth, then profitability, and ultimately loss of the right to exist.[2]

We reap what we sow, and there is a high cost of discount culture. Consumers have always loved a good deal. But that love has evolved into a somewhat destructive obsession.[3]

The agenda of this chapter is clear. In the long run, commoditization will be the major economic issue. Consequently, revised business models are required. Their output should be value creation, with a predominant emphasis on the customer side. Innovation and implementation are keys to business development. Success will depend on the competencies of market-oriented executives with new managerial profiles and a will to make customer satisfaction their top priority.

This chapter not only provides an in-depth definition of commoditization and its business consequences; it also dispels myths surrounding commoditization, which result too often in an incoherent set of strategic responses.

A New Economic Reality: More, Cheaper, Faster, and Profitable!

Let us start with an incredibly passé premonition. In 1943, two years before the end of World War II, Winston Churchill declared, "What the world needs now is a good 5 cent cigar." During this stressful period, the strong yearning for relief in general and for peace in particular is easily understandable. Let's focus on the key words he used and how they are connected. The first one is "world." He was not speaking about a specific country, such as the United Kingdom. The geographical framework is the entire world; it is "global." The second important word is "good." People are expecting a good cigar. They want a pleasurable customer experience, not a standard one. But the price has to be low: 5¢! Here is the winning formula: the cigar has to be good at a very low price. Just because the price is low, the cigar should not be cheap and consequently of poor quality. The fourth significant word—"now"—sounds like another express requirement: people do not want to wait for the expected cigar. They seek fast, easy access. Putting all these words together, we get the description of a low-cost, high-value type of commercial offer for a cigar, combined with total and fast access.[4] You have to admit that Winston Churchill was either a keen futurologist or a precocious business innovator. Did he even realize it? At any rate, this spontaneous statement remains highly pertinent today.

A few years ago, Andrea Jung, then Avon's CEO, confirmed this premonition and translated it into business language by applying it to her own sector: "The game of beauty is changing so much. If your product isn't high tech or can't make a unique performance claim—plump your lips, reduce your lines, look glossy, and stay on for 24 hours—you can't go to market today. I am not just talking about a $20 lipstick, but a $5 lipstick! We have spent about $100 million on a new R&D center."

The business rules of market launch and delivery are identical in both examples, even if they belong to vastly different eras, situations, and fields. They both concern delivery of more benefits to the customer, with higher quality, faster delivery, and easy access, all at a lower price. This is the extreme opposite of a traditional and conservative vision linking top quality to higher price and to selective distribution, the former way of creating perceived rarity.

Two interrelated yet potentially opposite characteristics are huge investments in product development and the unavoidable quest for the resulting profitability. Will both margins and sales volume be sufficient to cover such investments? Margins are rightly under scrutiny. The creation of a "high-tech" lipstick, whatever this means, requires a huge investment.

These new business requirements are not only constraining; they are also universal. They apply to all economic sectors, from services to industry. Online financial services must generate more revenues per customer while costing less. Industrial products are under severe pressure, too. Hospitals are also under scrutiny; radical surgery is on its way. Is it possible for a hospital to slash costs and deliver high-quality care as it innovates? Yes, such a situation exists.[5]

The scissor effect is at play: what can you do when you cannot sufficiently raise your list prices during a period of strong inflation that affects the prices of your raw materials? Will you be able to pass the price increases along to your client? How will the final consumer react?

Even the very best performers in branding consumer goods, Coca-Cola, for example, cannot escape the threat of the scissor effect. In 2008, the newly elected CEO of Coca-Cola, Muhtard Kent, believed that a U.S. recession, which he considered likely, would hurt his business (he was right). He added that his fourth-quarter results could be dented by high commodity prices. This statement shows how a global leader in brand equity management is constantly preoccupied with commoditization, in this case at the production cost level. The focus is on the cost of "real" commodities (i.e., raw components of the "secret" recipe).

Another good example is Heidelberg, a worldwide leader in top-quality German industrial printing equipment. For many years, their competitive situation was very comfortable, deservedly so. Industrial buyers had to pay a substantial premium for Heidelberg equipment. Sales negotiation was limited. Industrial buyers who questioned the higher-than-the-competition pricing were systematically told, "Because we are Heidelberg." The company's approach was "take it or leave it." Over time, however, more competitors appeared, particularly from Japan. Their products were not necessarily as good as those of Heidelberg, but they were comparable. The only difference, a huge one, was price: the new competitors' products were much more affordable. Slowly but surely, these rivals gained market share points. Heidelberg had a hard time adapting internally and externally. They were so sure of their technical superiority. The CEO quickly realized that Heidelberg was in reactive mode and would have to fight commoditization. The CEO initiated a radical change in attitudes and practices among all employees. The move has been extremely painful. Some long-time employees did not understand the development of low-cost, high-value offers, backed by the marketing of solutions to customers as opposed to providing products designed by engineers strictly to please engineers. Perceiving organizational prostitution, many quit in frustration. The survival of the entire organization was at stake, but it overcame its hurdles. Business is back on track, though the struggle continues. The level of hypercompetition is even worse now than it was at the time of the initial crisis a few years ago.

We are living and working in a totally new economic world. The markets will not adapt to fit the business practices of the companies that supposedly serve them. In fact, the reverse is true. If you resist, you will at best stagnate or disappear unceremoniously. To quote the sadly missed Peter Drucker, "Be good, or get out!" Granted, this position is brutal, but new economic realities are less pliant than ever. A lack of competence at the top will have strong negative social consequences for an organization and its stakeholders. Executives need to fully assume their responsibilities and duties. Peter Drucker was absolutely right!

A World of Collisions

It is evident that today's business world is extremely unstable. It resembles a permanent storm characterized by a set of collisions that have merged on all markets at an increasing pace. Some collisions might occur more gradually than others depending on the sector. The force of the storm also varies. Every business sector will have to face it at some point.

Because these collisions are crucial in business, they deserve explanation. Here they will be examined individually, and their combined effects, which exacerbate and accelerate commoditization, will be discussed.

Collision #1: Critical Price

Initially, the retail price of a disruptive technology is always very high. Consider the list price of the first LCD flat-screen TVs, about

$20,000. Of course, this price will quickly decline, sometimes plunging by nearly half each year. Because of the cross-elasticity between the sales volume and the average list price of a SKU (stock keeping unit), the demand tends to increase at a slower rate until the price reaches a point of inflection, a critical list price, at which customers will perceive that the product is finally accessible. They then will begin to buy it en masse. Suddenly, sales are booming and demand soars (see figure 1.1). The critical price can be compared to a psychological price threshold, below which large numbers of potential buyers are suddenly ready to buy a product or a service. It is a way to cross the chasm from highly innovative products aimed at limited markets to highly diffused products reaching the mass market.[6, 7] Markets are thus moving from specialties to commodities. For example, the critical retail price for a digital camera went down to about $499; such an affordable price boosted sales, not profits.

Crossing the chasm has mainly been described as a desirable move. In practical terms, it is not necessarily so. As soon as the chasm is successfully crossed, premium prices tend to disappear. Competition on price then increases constantly. Once you have stepped straight into the commodity trap, you will have to adapt as fast as you can to a radically new competitive reality.

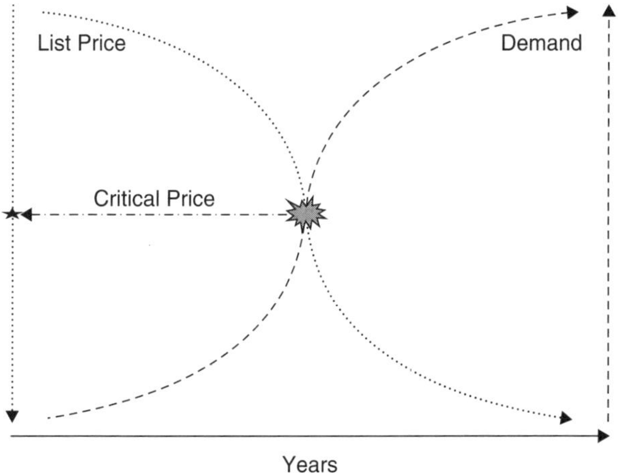

Figure 1.1 The critical list (or retail) price (A theoretical perspective).

Collision #2: Critical Mass

If the new product or service is a potential success, the next question is how much time will it need to reach the critical mass market? Nowadays, the average adoption (or diffusion) rate of any successful marketing concept is shortening. In fact, adoption rates at record speeds are becoming the rule in particularly turbulent product categories, such as DVD players and even high-definition television sets. Remember, it took nearly 15 years for color TV to reach the mass market (from 1955 to 1970). The introduction phase of the product life cycle was extremely long. In stark contrast, the success of DVD players was so instantaneous that the introduction phase of its life cycle was simply bypassed. The spread of products into households is speedier than ever.

The first theoretical consequence is that the traditional innovation adoption curve must be revised (see figure 1.2). The so-called normal curve tends to be skewed more and more to the left. Most often, it becomes quite abnormal. This radical shift is caused by new business practices. It is crucial for companies to learn how to manage their product and service portfolios properly. The aim is to preserve an optimal balance between specialties and commodities. Specifically, the game is to maximally protect specialties and use them as cash cows.

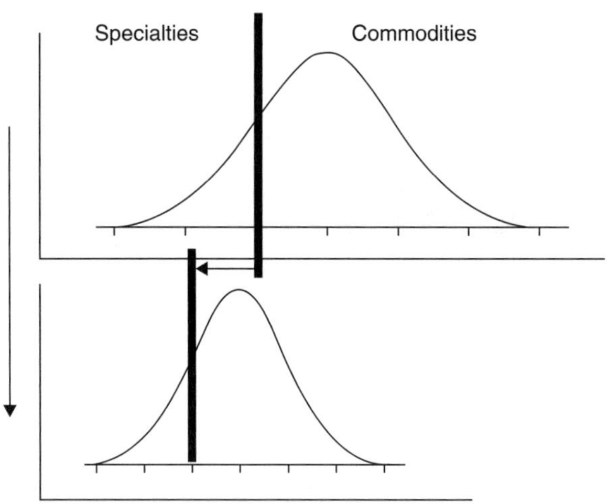

Figure 1.2 Diffusion curve revised.

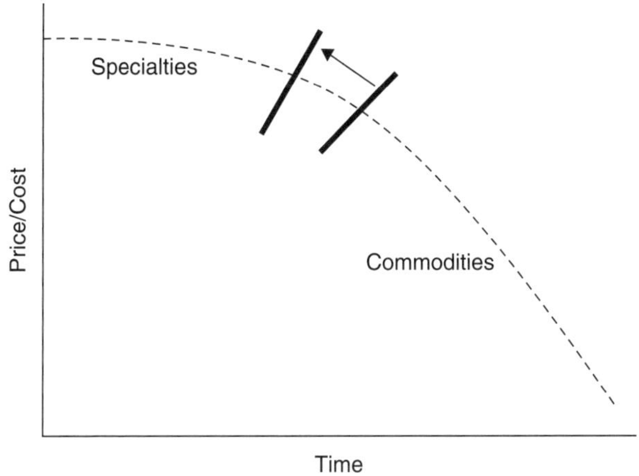

Figure 1.3 Learning how to sell commodities with profits.

Executives must also learn how to generate profits from commodities. This challenge has been well understood and executed by Dell, for example (see figure 1.3). As long as they were the only player in their sector to manage this challenge effectively, both their differentiation and their competitive edge were assured. Several years later, competitors learned how to match or even surpass their competencies. A few years ago, Michael Dell gave many conferences to MBA students around the world. He would stress how surprised he was that so many students were reading case studies of his direct, low-cost business model but that nobody had been able to reproduce it yet. He was somewhat cynical during his heyday. Now his comments have come back to haunt him. Dell, too, has fallen into the commodity trap.

The same pattern can also be seen in the mobile phone sector, in which the adoption rates of new technologies are accelerating: the adoption rate of 1G technology was fast but nowhere near as fast as 2G, and 3G has been even faster! The Japanese market, dominated by NTT Docomo, is a perfect example of this phenomenon. The number of NTT Docomo subscribers is increasing at a faster and faster rate with every launch of a new technology. Another noteworthy type of increased speed is the time frame of new product or service development, which is different from the diffusion rate. It is the next collision on which we will focus, called time-to-market.

Collision #3: Critical Time-to-Market

To review our last example, NTT Docomo, the time to develop a new concept (in this case a new technology) has decreased sharply over the years.

Enormous pressure is being put on R&D departments to feed the frenetic race for innovation. Some companies are even developing an internal culture of perpetual crisis. Samsung exemplified this policy for many years: don't predict the future, invent the future! It sounds good. The problem is how to sustain this constant pressure on your troops over time. If you try hard to push a competitor out of the market with speedy innovation as your strategic weapon, there is a high probability that, sooner or later, another competitor will do the same thing to you. It is not surprising that one of the main issues experts are working on is maintaining the momentum.[8]

For example, Samsung fought hard against Sony, quite successfully. Now LG is putting the same pressure on Samsung, and Samsung is suffering. Which (Chinese?) company will be the next to chase LG's tail? The sequence of reciprocal pressure is never-ending, and the stakes are constantly rising.

This race for time-to-market is extremely demanding. It might also affect overall quality. Many companies, especially in the software industry, are launching products that are permanent works-in-progress, to the chagrin of their final users. Microsoft Vista software is plagued by perpetual problems. It has now lost trust internally and externally. Launching unfinished products drives the commoditization process because it tarnishes overall consumer perceptions. Skepticism prevails. Both Microsoft and the final users are hoping Windows 7 will solve the problems once and for all. Microsoft must not fail again. Telling customers you do not "support" a product anymore because a new one is coming down the pipeline is the ideal way to stoke frustration and drag your customer satisfaction index down. And what can we say about the humbling of Toyota? A combination of high-speed global growth and ambitious cost cuts led to the quality lapses that have seriously tarnished the once-mighty brands of Toyota and Lexus.[9, 10]

Finally, decreasing the time-to-market and increasing disruptive innovations (including technologies) reinforces commoditization. If you innovate, in a relatively short time frame, on each of the attributes of your products or services, you quickly eliminate product differentiation because innovations become banal. Clearly, product differentiation alone cannot singly drive growth and stock performance. Companies fiercely engaged in hypercompetition are burning the candle at both ends. From an objective standpoint, do they have a choice?

Collision #4: Critical Displacement

As soon as a disruptive technology successfully crosses the chasm, it will quickly replace the old one. Two important rules appeared in a major article in 1995.[11] First, when a disruptive technology meets the performance demands of mainstream customers, the customers will switch to it, even it is inferior to the sustaining technology. Second, supply quality improves more quickly than demand requires.

Let's take a simple example to illustrate those two rules. When they reached the price threshold, digital cameras did not exceed 3.1 megapixels. Nevertheless, the technical performance of this disruptive technology was sufficient for mainstream consumers, despite the fact that it was obviously far from the quality definition of traditional film photography (the old technology). Digital cameras have since been inserted in mobile phones, creating a new concept: camera phones. During the introduction phase, the image definition was about 1.1 megapixels. They were fun to use. Final users were not concerned with taking professional-quality pictures. The technology improved fast, however, and now mobile phones are competing directly with digital cameras. There is significant negative cross-elasticity between the sales of both products. Displacement is not at 100 percent because mobile phones have not entirely replaced digital cameras yet, but the increase in the sales of camera phones flattened the sales of digital cameras. Now some digital cameras deliver 15 megapixels!

This process is repeating itself endlessly. What is remarkable is that most often, companies that were the leaders in an old industry are unable to maintain their position when a disruptive technology emerges. Generally, they (almost) disappear because by the time they recognize the threat and take it seriously, it is too late. Kodak is a striking example. It was considered a major blue chip on the stock exchange for many years—not anymore. Polaroid suffered the same fate.

The impact of a disruptive technology is not limited to the tangible (i.e., a product and its technical performance). It might also severely impact intangibles, namely services, in particular the simultaneous production and delivery of a service. In the marketing of the intangible, service and distribution are indissociable. That is how the Internet has killed the traditional brick-only travel agency in the United States.

Slowly but surely, this radical transformation is spreading around the world. Voice-Over Internet telephone (VOIP) is another example of a service provided by the Internet, as is satellite radio. One key strategic issue in the world of media (content and transportation) is television over the Internet or Internet Protocol Television (or IPTV). A large company like Microsoft is betting heavily on it. It is a strategic stake for them. They see it as a possible rebound (or revenge) against the overwhelming spread of Google's search engines, control of individual information, and online advertising. Sometimes there is a displacement between the tangible and the intangible parts of a commercial offer. In the music industry, sales of CDs are falling steadily. At the same time, sales from downloading music are rising. In software, the de-materialization of products is building momentum. People have stopped buying specific software in the packaging format of a CD or a DVD inserted in a cardboard box. They increasingly connect to a specific Web site and download the product. The major recording labels such as Sony Music Entertainment, Universal Music Group, Warner Music Group, and EMI, the packaging industry, and the mass retailers must reposition themselves. A sweeping transformation is affecting all of their business models.

Collision #5: Critical Price Nears Zero

Not only will the performance of a new technology increase every year, but its price will fall simultaneously. Take computer chips and the famous Moore's Law (the number of transistors on a chip will double about every two years). It is extremely attractive at first glance. Executing it, however, could be a business nightmare (see figure 1.4).

What is incredible is that the continuous, spectacular development of a disruptive technology has a matching inverse pattern related to price. Companies are offering more and more in terms of product or service performance at an even lower price. It is precisely what Avon's CEO said (at the beginning of this chapter). Au contraire, simply adding extra performance to your product—be it a computer, hotel stay, or lipstick—does not mean you can automatically apply a premium.

The final result of these two patterns, from a consumer perspective, is that you can now buy a digital camera, with a recognized brand name and image definition twice as high as two years ago, at a price half of that of two years ago. Think about it. Most consumers do not realize how serious the business and social consequences of this collision are! The pressure on developers is enormous. Increasing productivity

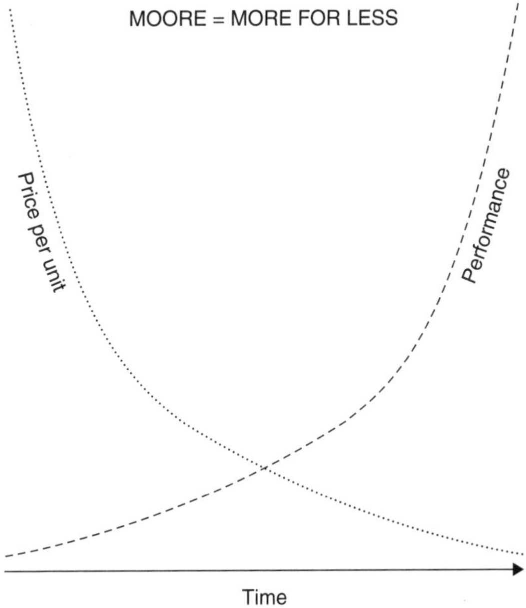

Figure 1.4 Moore's Law (Performance and cost).

constantly is crucial as a response to such demanding requirements. Some companies are up to the challenge. Others just throw in the towel. They stay in business as long as they can improve performance at a profit. For example, in the fierce race for flat-screen TV sets, Pioneer is running out of gas.

In some sectors, the price nears zero. Some visionaries are seeing "free as the future of a radical price."[12] This can apply to selling activities in sectors such as phones, magazines, newspapers, and even pop singers. For example, some companies are delivering their products for free. By bundling their free offer with peripheral services and a mid- or long-term binding contract, they expect to attract and retain consumers and maintain their profitability through an increase in usage. They are not trying to generate a profit from the purchasing act alone. The applicability of this extreme approach is not universal: it requires flexibility in execution. But it might be a clever solution to a dead end. Let's take another look at the music industry. Many people say pop stars should earn their money by performing more concerts and should not expect to earn as much income from CD sales (i.e., waiting passively for money to flow in). This is precisely what Prince did. He delivered one of his latest albums for free, as an insert in a newspaper. He then earned money by giving concerts based on the new album. Although the newspaper lost money during the launch, it earned a positive ROI. In the end, the move was a very sound advertising investment and not an expense at all—a real "win-win" situation.

More recently, in an official announcement made in July 2009, Microsoft said it would offer a free version of its popular Office software that could run on the Internet. It clearly looks like a major strategic move that will allow Microsoft to protect its most profitable businesses against Google.

Critical Combined Effects (1+2+3+4 = Commoditization)

None of these collisions happens in isolation. They act simultaneously and produce reinforced effects. The pace of innovation is increasing: both time-to-market and time to reach critical mass are plunging, and mass markets are developing faster than ever, while prices are decreasing. Most often, new products go on special almost immediately after being launched on worldwide markets, or even before. This is particularly true of electronics such as digital cameras, DVD players, and even LCD televisions. Consumers should not be seen as the only cause of this odd situation. Many companies hastily discount prices instead of charging a premium price for new products and services. Such incoherent practices are very short-term oriented and are basically conditioned and irrational business reflexes. They are building loyalty to low prices and promotions while eroding the differentiation and uniqueness effect. It is a real pity.

Of course, the relative increase in the appearance of disruptions instead of incremental improvements is adding to the turbulence. The effect of successive incremental improvements is much smoother than that of disruptive technologies. The pace of the appearance of disruptions is increasing and is driving commoditization. For instance, the battle between standards is raging in the electronics sector. LCD and plasma televisions are still fighting, but there is a clear advantage for LCD technology.

Large electronics companies are already seeing the advent of flexible display screens fast approaching. Here again, different standards arise for the same concept: transform a TV screen into a poster that can be rolled up, transported easily, and hung anywhere. Or transform a book into an electronic display through an electronic ink process (HP, DuPont,

Xerox, Philips, and many other big players have already entered this race). Dr. Alan Heeger received a Nobel Prize in chemistry in 2000 for his research into tapping the power of plastic. Plugged-in polymers are already being transformed into rollable LCDs; the commercial battle has begun. The prices of the first plastic screens are extremely high, of course, but they will decrease as the technology improves. Some supposedly innovative products might already be "out-of-date." One example is the Kindle (the electronic book) that Jeff Bezos, Amazon's CEO, is trying hard to launch after the successful launch of the iPad from Apple. Is it the right format for a digital book? Some people are comparing it with a real book. Obviously, the feel is not the same. There are likely other issues, too. The current digital format, even improved, is probably just a "concept-in-progress."

The Commoditization Conundrum

James Surowiecki said, in 1998:

> If there's one thing that microeconomics has demonstrated it is that it's hard to keep your profit margins high if you are in the wheat-growing business. Wheat is pretty much wheat, no matter where it grows, and it's pretty easy to grow unless the Dust Bowl is raging. That means that the supply of wheat rises quickly to meet demand, which in turn, is the definition of a commodity, and the market for wheat—absent government intervention—is almost as close to perfect as you can imagine.[13]

At first glance, this statement depicts commoditization as a microeconomic phenomenon that is clear and easy to understand. In reality, commoditization is not an easy concept to describe. It will be defined below from different perspectives, using Sony as the best example of how a large, renowned company can get caught in the commodity trap. One of these is an enlarged business perspective, focusing on its main causal effects, followed by its social aspect in the buying decision process and its managerial consequences.

Shakeup at Sony (and More)

For many years, the name Sony was synonymous with superior, innovative products. Suddenly, at the end of the previous century, their profitability dropped precipitously.[14] The CEO himself admitted to the business media that his company was suffering from a severe case of the large company disease commoditization. He then resigned. A close look at Sony's balance sheet confirmed the diagnosis. Most of their income came from electronics devices. It was precisely in this product line that Sony was losing money. New products were being reduced to commodities too quickly and were selling for less than they would otherwise. The uphill battle for recovery is not over. Sony's new boss, who is exceptionally not Japanese (and this is quite a revolution considering that it stands against the tradition of viewing strangers as dangers), is still hoping for a revival. Unfortunately, rediscovering the magic formula is not a given. The profile of the new economic reality is far removed from Sony's highly conservative internal cultural pattern. Sony's rebirth is complicated even more by the severity of the current recession. They believe now that the worst is behind them and that their new products—especially those involving 3D technologies—will make quite a splash.[15, 16]

This case is not unique. Companies of all sizes are suffering from the same disease; it is a virtual pandemic. Even large companies working in more protected markets are beginning to feel the commoditization effect. For example, big manufacturers of selective brands of cosmetics and luxury apparel such as high-end clothes and expensive watches must cope with this reality. Even pharmaceutical companies are not immune. The battle against generic drugs is closely linked to the worldwide commoditization process.

Commoditization: The Major Threat to Differentiation

Commoditization is the inexorable transformation of unique goods and services into commodities. It leads to a total lack of differentiation between the offers in a specific sector. For example, there is a perception that there are no differences between the brands of high-end LCD TV sets, between the mortgages offered by different financial institutions, between the business propositions of industrial contractors, between large steel suppliers, and so forth. When the customers or industrial buyers perceive all offers as the same, then their only buying criterion, or basis of selection among available brands or suppliers, is price. The product or service offered need not be a basic commodity per se (such as a raw material). As long as it is "perceived" as undifferentiated, it transforms itself into a commodity according to the strict economic definition and automatically joins the ranks of commodities with its exclusively price-driven competitive behaviors.

Technically speaking, commoditization is a market process that affects the role of the brand (as a buying criterion) in the customer's decision-making process, regardless of its presence or necessity.[17] It does not imply the demise of the brands, as warned by experts, especially gurus wanting to spread hype. It does decrease the expected returns from a strong brand policy as a result of two related issues. First, it drastically limits the capacity and freedom of a manufacturer or service provider to apply a systematic pricing premium to an offer with unique added value. A strong brand no longer guarantees a price premium. Second, it transforms absolute brand loyalty into shared brand loyalty among an evoked set of comparable brands, a well-known megatrend occurring worldwide and across product/service categories. It leads to the erosion and potential disappearance of exclusivity and proprietary business privileges. Paradoxically, from an ironic standpoint, commoditization represents the development of a socialist approach in a pure capitalist arena.

Commoditization as a Lack of Relationship

From an environmental and social perspective, a commodity is an object outside of oneself, a thing whose qualities satisfy a human. It is a useful thing, but mostly it is a thing, not a relationship.[18] The lack of relationship between the thing (a product or a service) and the client is important because it is a potential source of disengagement among buyers and an explanation for the increase in the number of people switching brands, distributors, mass distributors, and so on.

Obviously, the commoditization process occurs differently in product or service categories. Goods and services can be described as having high commodity potential (HCP) or low commodity potential (LCP), depending mainly on their suitability for mass production and distribution.

Commoditization has two major consequences. First, it can be defined along a continuum, with different products and services ranging from high to low commoditization potential. Second, directly related to the previous consequence, rebuilding a relationship between products or services and the targeted consumers will be more or less straightforward, depending on whether the brand belongs to the mass or the selective market. Cult brands are a different story. These issues will be explored in detail later (in chapter 6).

Remember, nothing is impossible. Even for a very basic commodity, in an extreme case of a total absence of relationship, it is still possible to create uniqueness. Specialty salt is a good example. The product might be handmade, organic, or even protected by a label of origin. The final result is the selling of a selective salt at a sizeable premium. Salt is not salt anymore.

Commoditization as a Loss of Managerial Control

From a general managerial perspective, commoditization means a present and future loss of control by companies over their business assets, that is, their brands and financial returns and, ultimately, their potential survival. (A typical question is "What does our future as a bank, travel agency, academic institution, scientific journal, car dealer, etc., hold?"). Business equity is on shaky ground.

All these effects are creating real nightmares not only for marketing experts but also for many corporate executives, especially those who sell products or services that were not previously associated with commodity markets but are now deeply engaged in them. The commoditization process is in its growth phase. It is here to stay and will not fade away.

We need to take a closer look at the causes of this long-term, irreversible economic development. Because of the severity of the recession, desperate attempts to reinstall protectionism might surface, but the political order of large economic markets has been clearly and firmly established. It is designed to facilitate open exchanges and free competition. This is why it is important to understand the economic mechanisms underlying the business world.

The Descriptive Model of Commoditization

Globalization and digitization are jointly fueling the commoditization process. Their major consequences are located either on the supply side or the demand side. Of course, subsequent consequences might appear, such as cross impacts on both sides. In order to keep the focus on the major economic issues, I simplify the picture and limit the number of causal relationships.

The major impact of globalization—brand proliferation—is on the supply side. By comparison, the major impact of digitization affects the demand side: customer empowerment (see figure 1.5). Together they explain the major shift in the overall configuration of brand choice behavior in the last 20 years. Specifically, there is a much larger choice of brands on the supply side; many more comparisons among available

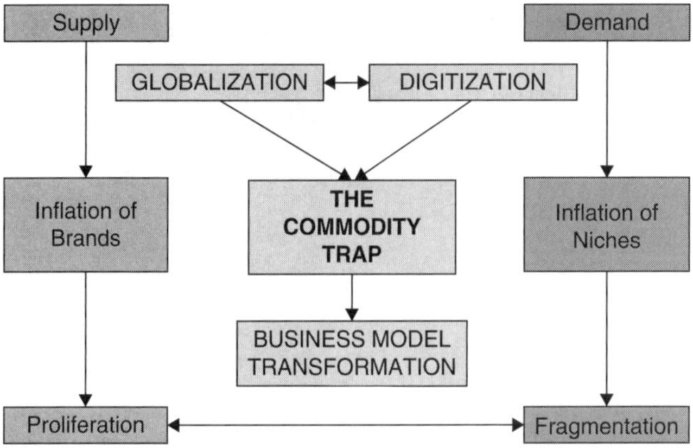

Figure 1.5 Globalization and digitization as the two main sources of commoditization.

and accessible brands; and a resulting decline in absolute brand loyalty, which is translated into greater difficulty maintaining margins and the overall financial performance of a company.

Let's start with the supply side. Several years ago, somebody who wanted to buy a pair of shoes in a small town had a limited choice: one general store, perhaps two, and a very limited selection of brands per store. Another way to buy this item was the traditional mail-order catalog. Nowadays, the same customer is probably connected to the Internet and has access to a large set of online stores, domestic or foreign (who cares anymore?), with a nearly unlimited selection of brands and models. The same situation applies to industrial goods. Globalization has positioned the customer in a perfect competitive setting. Monopolies have been abolished. The choice is yours: bricks only (physical storefronts), click only (online stores), or bricks and clicks.

The basic economic rule of supply and demand applies. The greater the choice, the more clients increase their expectations and the more extensively they bargain during the buying process. They will demand a zero-defect offer at a "fair price," which implies requesting higher quality at a lower price. This is known as the more-for-less paradigm. Over the years, people learn to negotiate more effectively. This system can be called the global factory (see figure 1.6). It is a continuous, irreversible learning curve. Customers are clamoring for more, more, more!

Globalization means the proliferation of brands and an infinite extension of the limits of choice. The consequence is obvious: brand dilution.

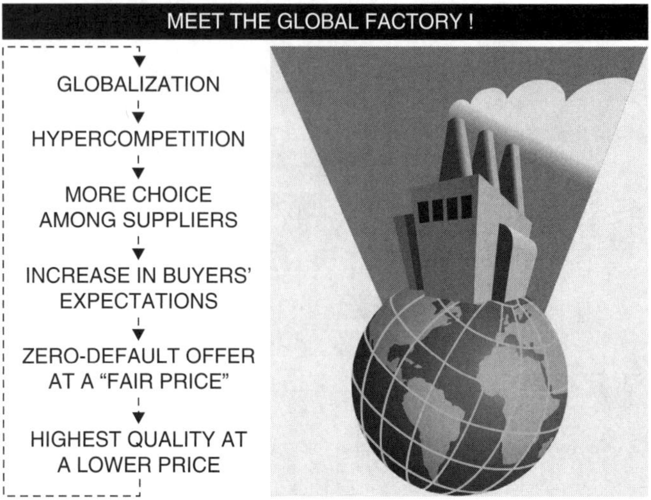

Figure 1.6 The globalization factory as a learning cycle.

Many brands are landing in customers' backyards. Competition is giving way to hypercompetition. To add to the complexity, the number of counterfeit products is also on the rise. Both gray and parallel markets are becoming well organized, with their own codes and rules. They are creating different levels of competitive market structures, in direct competition, and building efficient underground economies.

On the demand side, consumer empowerment is mounting. Clicking a mouse button is an easy way to surf around and, during online shopping activities, to comparison shop conveniently and intensively. The consumer is in control because the power has shifted along the distribution channel from manufacturers to distributors to final customers.

For many years, marketing experts insisted that the customer was the boss. We all assumed the customer was a "rabbit" and companies were hunters. The consumer was thus both target and boss. The problem is that today, the rabbit holds the rifle and is hunting for companies. Some people are happy because the customer finally is the boss. Their delight might be premature, though, because the commercial hunt has been reversed. The customer is becoming more and more aware of business practices because of easy access to information. Online transparency is a reality. People's fear that intense data collection is making the consumer naked is justified. However, companies are equally vulnerable. Many customers who enter the car dealership showroom are already aware of the technical issues related to the model they are looking for, and they know the price they should pay. People who say the impact of the Internet on the car industry is overstated because the market share of clients buying a car online is very limited are short-sighted. The focus should shift to the "information search" phase, which immediately precedes the "buying" phase in the consumer's decision process. These people will then notice that search activities are extremely intense and that a very large majority of potential buyers surf from manufacturer sites to dealer sites to independent sites in search of diverse information. If, as a brand manufacturer, you are not doing so well during the "information search" phase, do not be surprised if your sales are lower than projected. Where there's smoke, there's fire.

The next chapter discusses the consequences of these impacts on customers' attitudes and behaviors. These new attitudes and behaviors are creating new market dynamics and transforming the role of the brand. They are completely rewriting the rules of business, and companies must adapt to this new environment. Far too many companies and executives are reluctant to change. Even worse, some of the companies speak about the new realities but do not act accordingly. The necessary moves apply to others, not to them, of course.

The Two Major Megatrends in the Economy

At the turn of the millennium, many business students and executives were fed up with hearing about the so-called "new" economy. Experts heralded its appearance at the beginning of the dot.com era, but this trend was scuttled by the NASDAQ crash. Some experts then backpedaled and adopted what might be called an "I told you so" attitude. They argued that the Internet was hype only and would surely fade away. Only a limited number of courageous people resisted the short-term backlash, believing that everybody else was dreaming, and insisted that digitization would have a highly significant, long-term impact on business operations. They rightly did not change their minds and attitudes based on the ever-shifting winds in the business world. They discovered that a new economy was being woven, which implies a new setting for business, and that more time was needed to manage the overall change. Just as a tanker can't make a U-turn on a dime, neither can the global economy. A new reality has set in, and here are the two megatrends that characterize it.

(Very) Low-Cost Business Models

Many labels have been used for new business models that advocate rigorous management of customer expectations and delivery of high added value paired with low cost. At first, the "low-cost" expression was used mainly to describe a new type of airline, such as Southwest Airlines, Jet Blue, and Easy Jet. Now the term is becoming more generic and is widely used across industries. The "more-for-less" customer request is being integrated into the basic structure of companies.

The dual effect of globalization and digitization is not only at the crux of the commoditization process; it is also the economic source of the low-cost business models and their endless rise (see figure 1.7).

Globalization and digitization have jointly created the perfect economic environment for the growth of the low-cost business models. Globalization is the fertile soil, and digitization is the fertilizer. This context is the visible manifestation of commoditization from a business practice perspective. Low-cost business models are proliferating. Very low-cost, instead of low-cost, business models are even emerging. The increased pressure to perpetually lower costs reflects the principle of communicating vessels on the global economic scale,[19] specifically the current process of rebalancing PPP (purchase power parity) between the so-called incumbents and emerging economies. If one side is going

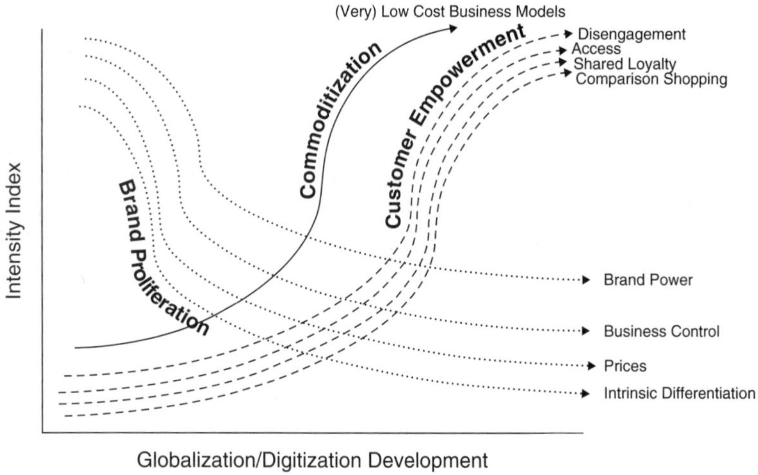

Figure 1.7 The weaving of a (real) new economy.

up, the other should go down. The question is whether the process will stop smoothly at the equilibrium. It will probably take a long time to stabilize.

Let us look at famous examples from two disparate sectors. The first one, in consumer services, involves the comeback of McDonald's at Starbucks' expense; and the second concerns the race to build very cheap cars.

Starbucks' famous business model is under heavy attack. In early 2009, they had to close thousands of stores and fire thousands of employees. The reasons for this huge setback generated much discussion. The fact that they opened too many stores is an oft-repeated argument: remember the famous joke about the opening of a new Starbucks in the Starbucks. There is another good explanation: commoditization. Slowly but surely, they lost their uniqueness in their core activity: specialty coffees. This sparked the famous controversy over the $4 "Frappucino." The threat has come from an unexpected mass-market competitor, McDonald's. McDonald's is not only recession resistant, but they are also a very aggressive competitor. They know how to make money by selling commodities. This managerial skill may not be as cultivated in the more "selective" culture prevailing at Starbucks, which is too bad! McDonald's quickly acquired new high-tech coffee machines that can produce "Ice Mochas" at a low cost, namely a price roughly half that of the Frappucino. Many not-so-loyal customers, more sensitive to price than to the "coffee experience," switched over. To hammer in their supremacy, McDonald's brazenly posted an outdoor advertisement near Starbucks' head office arguing that paying four bucks for espresso is dumb. The fairness of this strategy may be debatable, but it worked. Online buzz marketing took up the slack, multiplying, for free, both the impact of the message and the total size of the audience.

The second example is the rise of low-cost cars. Are they cheap cars? Is this the real issue? When a very large and highly diversified company like Tata of India launched the Nano, it might have been perceived as "cheap" because its basic equipment is designed to meet the low requirements of the company's domestic market, coupled with a rock-bottom price to make it accessible to people with very limited budgets. When the initial product is revamped and adapted to the needs of more "sophisticated" markets, in the European community, for example, then the cheap car becomes a low-cost product. Even if the price increased from about 1,500 Euros in India to 5,000

Euros in Europe, it is still a good deal. Many European consumers might be attracted to such cars because their purchasing power is decreasing. Of course, the competition will soon step up to the plate. Renault is already playing the game with the Dacia Logan. They tout it as the best cheap car in the world. Their model can be considered a "super budget automobile." Just because you are playing in the low-cost league doesn't mean you can afford to neglect your image. Toyota is designing low-cost cars for Russia. Volkswagen will assemble their low-cost models in Russia. Nissan is planning new low-cost small cars for Brazil, and China is coming out with the QQ. After years of making their mass-market cars more expensive, the world's automakers have abruptly shifted into reverse. The situation is quite urgent. The car has become a commodity to an unprecedented degree. Emergent countries might be in a better position to profit from this trend because they can surf the wave of commoditization. Ratan Tata, the chairman of the Tata Group, expects to sell 250,000 to 500,000 Nanos a year, as of 2010–2011. In contrast, this business reinvention is harder for the "Detroit Three" and for GM in particular. The Tata way has nothing to do with the GM way. Remarkably, though, all these car makers are asking their governments for bailouts.

The "Wikification" of the Economy

In 2007, at Davos, Swiss businessman, economist, and philanthropist Klaus Schwab affirmed that the most important issue facing the economy will be the power shift from the center to the periphery. Vertical-and-control structures are being eroded and replaced by (online) communities and different (open) platforms. He added that we are moving into the Web 2.0 world, which has tremendous implications on business models, at the national level. In 2009, the gathering at Davos was gloomier, for obvious reasons. Executives from around the world were preoccupied with the recession. The ambiance at Davos aside, it is important to remember that commoditization and the recession are closely related.

The worldwide opening of international borders has created large markets and a giant trade platform where everything is connected.[20] First came the Internet revolution, then the wireless revolution. Wireless technology links not just people, allowing them to exchange information from anywhere in the world, but also objects. With the development of the semantic world, machines can also communicate directly. This might be tremendously useful, but it is harder to achieve than businesses might think.

"From a business perspective, a comparative advantage cannot be counted on to create [...] net gains greater than the net losses from trade (Paul Samuelson, MIT)." Commoditization proneness as applied to the content of commercial offers (brands, products, services, distribution channels, and low prices) is putting extreme pressure on brands, and they must be on their guard.

In their first edition of each year, *Time* magazine highlights the person of the year. In 2007, there was a mirror on the cover page, with a title: "You." [21] *Time* was telling people around the world that they control the information age. Now it's your turn. The huge development of social networks and online communities is a new reality. Nearly everyone has a friend online, who is a friend of a friend, and so on. This is a tremendous revolution. The problem is that online communities have nothing to do with traditional communities in general and brand communities in particular. The famous but traditional Harley-Davidson brand community is not easily transferable and manageable in an online context. Online consumers are increasingly disengaged. They still consume, but they are less and less dependent on brand manufacturers.

The key business challenge is to figure out how to harness the power of masses of one,[22] to extract value from social "graph-iti,"[23] to benefit from prosumers instead of consumers, and to get crowd-sourcing right.[24, 25] The contribution revolution is taking shape. It is about participation, "ideagoras," collaboration, and placing a huge bet on collective intelligence, introduced with great fanfare in the "wiki-economy" (an open economy where mass collaboration changes everything through massive online communities).[26] It is an extreme challenge for traditional companies because it taps the contributions of countless people inside and outside organizations, peering collaboration in innovation among competitors, Internet leaders, and so on. It is putting system contribution to work on a worldwide basis with an open approach. It is sending huge shock waves through the business world. What's more, the "wiki" business approach does not follow the rules of business territory, decision disclosure, and especially total control by companies. This reversal is still in the introduction phase. In the near future, be vigilant and be ready to adapt. If you don't, then you will definitely stagnate.

In a nutshell, total access is replacing total control. Customer value creation at a very low cost is the major stake of this new competitive game. John G. Stumpf, Wells Fargo's chief executive, said in March 2009, "This downturn is different. It will define a generation." Truly, a new generation is emerging—in the economy, business practices, and leadership profiles. It centers on customer value creation.

CHAPTER 2

New Markets, New Behaviors: A Global Shift

> Marketers should prepare now for a possible long term shift in consumers' values and attitudes.
>
> —John A. Quelch and Katherine E. Jocz[1]

Everyone knows you have to change with your customers to win big.[2] This has always been true: typically, a marketing plan must be reworked, or at least reviewed, every year. The only difference between the landscape before and after the emergence of commoditization is that the changes in attitudes and behaviors among both consumers and industrial buyers are here to stay. Such changes are less connected to a fashionable business practice or a short-term market tendency than they used to be in many circumstances. The internal structure of the business world is being totally reconfigured. Executives must grasp not only the transformations to consumption patterns in the B2C markets but also those affecting B2B trade. Manufacturers, distributors, and other economic players will have to fine-tune their strategies accordingly.

Many publications have covered this topic. They offer advice on how to effectively run a company. The confusing part is that their external validity is not always known. (We will assume here that their internal validity has been confirmed beforehand.) They focus on incumbents, namely consumers in emerging countries, and their scope is limited to the new buying psychology. They might assert, in all honesty, that the new economy, or even the ongoing recession, will have a lasting impact on the way people shop. It certainly will! Then they discuss how North American retailers are being affected. Understanding the so-called "post-recession consumer" is a strategic priority.[3] Far too few publications embrace a real global vision of the reconfiguration of buying behaviors by showing how the decline in the developed economies might be counterbalanced by an upturn in emergent ones. A worldwide perspective could yield a more objective diagnosis of the global management of product or service portfolios. Some manufacturer brands are under attack in Europe and North America, whereas other brands are prospering in China, India, or Brazil. So what is the best way to assess large companies' competitive and financial situation on the global scale? Shifting consumption patterns are difficult to grasp. Strategies will hinge on which scenario materializes. For now, though, companies should do four things: prepare for slower long-term growth in global consumption, shift investments to Asia, focus on older consumers (in the United States, Europe, and Japan), and find ways to offer luxury on a budget.[4]

Another major concern is that researchers are sometimes using outdated concepts to analyze new market phenomena. Conceptual frameworks are always dependent, to some extent, on the economic context from which they spring and in which they are developed and refined. Here is a critical example, which we will revisit later in detail because it is directly linked to commoditization. Obviously, market polarization between the high-end tier of consumers and the low-end tier exists. Sales distribution has evolved largely between the two extremes. The most widely used framework of analysis is the traditional (and statistically monotonic) price-quality relationship: the higher the price, the better the quality. The problem is that this traditional perspective has been seriously undermined because the relationship is no longer linear. To analyze new trends in consumption data, an updated approach is essential. Unfortunately, not everyone agrees.

In addition, the real causes of recent attitudinal and behavioral changes in consumption and industrial buying may differ between B2B and B2C. Are we dealing with the basic effect of commoditization or that of a recession (or downturn)? Of course, commoditization and recessions are closely related, and every recession is unique. Because economic phenomena are intertwined, it is extremely difficult to measure the net effect of a particular economic contraction on evolving consumption and buying patterns. Cumulative effects also come into play. For example, many articles have dealt with the current severe recession and its impact. The idea is to help companies adapt—their existing strategies might propel or undermine their performance. In fact, there is a real need for more research into the long-term consequences of the recession, in particular its effect on an in-depth reconfiguration of business models. The well-timed publishing of short-term strategic recommendations is often incompatible with the need to take the time to fully grasp the phenomena and their long-term strategic consequences. It is clear that the recession will have a lasting impact on the way people shop.[5] Recession or not, American families will be forced to tighten their belts.[6] And this movement will extend to other developed countries, such as Canada.[7]

As if the economic analysis were not complex enough, the trends are not isolated. They are closely interrelated, and their effects are combined. There is a genuine ecosystem of concepts and their internal relationships. New conceptual frameworks show that the polarization of markets is closely related to the creation of a "mass-tige" market, in which the revised price-quality relationship is the main underlying conceptual explanation. New conceptual tools will improve our understanding of what is actually going on.

This chapter presents a balanced long-term view of the current trends in consumption and buying patterns. The focus is on the advanced economies, also known as the incumbents, but emerging economies will also be discussed. It is impossible to understand global business by examining only one side of the planet. One conceptual framework of analysis is highlighted: the traditional price-quality analysis. I cover the main transformations without going into detail. Digressions may be interesting in their own right but have limited strategic implications. This book performs a strategic analysis, not a tactical one.

The Vanishing Middle (or Mass?) Market

Analysis of new trends in consumer spending clearly shows that premium and no-frills offerings are squeezing out middle-of-the-road products and services in many industries. This new economic phenomenon is called market polarization. Is it caused by or closely related to commoditization? To answer this question, we must consider the drivers of commoditization that are affecting market patterns: new technology (digitization) and product proliferation (globalization). This combined impact was explained in chapter 1.

A clear definition of the concept of a vanishing "middle" or "mass" market is important here because two very different perspectives have been advanced. In strict economic terms, global data show that the growth rate of revenues for midtier products and services trailed the market average significantly, estimated at nearly 6 percent a year (measuring 25 industries and product categories in Europe, North

America, and the rest of the world).[8] Three tiers have been defined: a high end, with a growth rate of 8.7 percent above the average; a middle one, with negative growth of 5.7 percent; and a no-frills/value tier, growing at 4.2 percent, between 1999 and 2004. Premium and no-frills are squeezing-of-the road products and services. Changing customer needs are prompting a range of strategic responses. But the vanishing middle market does not stand for the vanishing mass market.[9] For marketers in the so-called "developed world", it means that the evolution from mass to micromarketing is a fundamental change driven as much by necessity (negative growth in the overall middle market) as opportunity (targeting the most valuable/high volume consumers or niches). And, in the developing world's increasingly prosperous consumer markets, multinational companies need new "scale at speed" approaches to capture the world's emerging class.[10]

Research points to significant variations in the way polarization plays out within industries. Industries can be segmented into three groups. In group 1, the polarization is quite balanced. For companies competing in industries and product categories as diverse as appliances, banking, mobile phones, and apparel, growth is strong at both ends of the market. Here the strategic choices are particularly difficult because they consist solely in trade-offs. It is hard for a company to create extra value and strip down at the same time. In contrast, group 2 companies, which include airlines, groceries, PCs, and server manufacturers, are migrating toward value-oriented parts of the market. For these firms, controlling costs is critical because they are constantly being attacked by no-frills competitors. In retail commerce, particularly in Europe, hard discounters are besetting the hypermarket model. For example, Carrefour, in France, is being threatened by the vigorous growth of the German Lidl, where "quality is cheaper." Group 3 comprises manufacturers of products such as digital cameras, MP3 players, and coffeemakers. They are achieving growth at the high end of the market. The iPod is an extreme example of how the MP3 game has changed. Polarization occurs at significantly different speeds in different parts of the world. The growth rates of high-end models in Europe have definitively overtaken their North American counterparts, but the no-frills tier is also growing fast in Europe. This is not surprising because consumers' purchasing power is declining quickly in the Old World.

Behind the vanishing "mass" market lies another phenomenon. It has nothing to do with the polarization of markets but consists instead of an increasing individualization of people, driving a major shift in marketing from a mass approach to a highly targeted, individual one. This major issue was embodied in *Time*'s 2007 person of the year: You![11] Community and collaboration are expanding on an unprecedented scale. Social networks are thriving on the million-channel Internet. Many large corporations, including Proctor & Gamble, are claiming that every one of their brands is targeted. This trend particularly affects communication: we are seeing a gradual reduction in investment in traditional mass marketing and an increase in online advertisements, fueled by search engines, which fosters the development of contextual advertising. Some companies may offer customization for all, the cornerstone of an individualized relationship approach, also called 1-2-1. Coca-Cola, American Express, and even Pfizer are trying to pick their targets carefully. We will revisit this issue later in this chapter, as it is a major and direct consequence of democratization and the increase in individual use of the Internet along with other digital technologies, such as the WiMAX.

The End of the Price-Quality Relationship: The Mass-tige Concept

As mentioned in the introduction of this chapter, many conceptual frameworks are obsolete. They no longer fit reality. Their external validity is at best questionable and at worst completely irrelevant.

One of the conceptual frameworks that are seriously being rethought is particularly relevant to marketing segmentation: the traditional price-quality relationship. It assumes that there is a positive and monotonic relationship between the price of a product or a service and its quality. This gives rise to two major segments of consumers or buyers: selective, namely people who are ready to pay more for higher quality; and mass, a cluster of people who are more price-sensitive and less quality-oriented. For many years, most markets have been divided in this way. The virtual absence of an overlap between the segments made marketing management quite simple. Some companies, or business units, were focusing on the high end of the market, others on the low end. Meanwhile, buyers were not expecting more for less. It was not part of their perception, nor were they used to it. Consequently, there was no significant market segment for high-value products or services at a low cost.

The ongoing development of commoditization has changed the picture dramatically. Now that more and more buyers have easy access to a wide range of alternative commercial offers, they have raised their

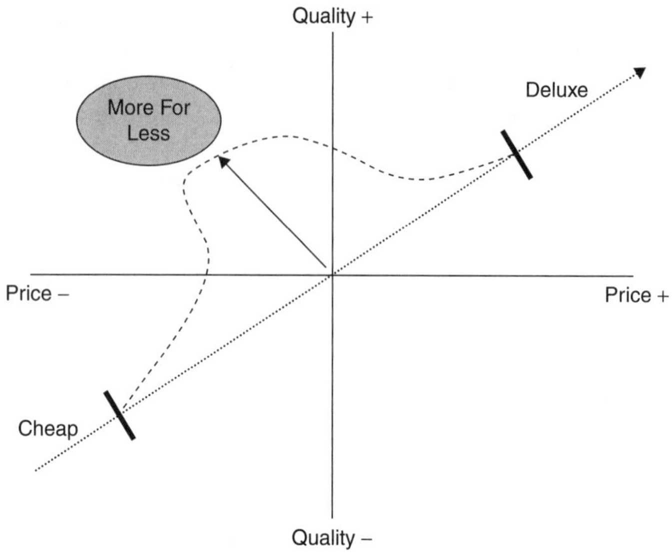

Figure 2.1 The biased price-quality relationship.

expectations and are demanding more at a better price. The linear price-quality relationship is no longer valid: it is biased and resembles an inclined normal curve, as a growing number of middle-market consumers trade up (see figure 2.1).

The traditional, exclusive polarization between the selective and the mass markets is over. The frontier between the top of the middle range and the bottom of the high range is blurry. There are obvious overlaps now. The future seems to lie in selective-mass products, or "mass-tige." This term is, of course, recently coined: it is formed from the words "mass" and "prestige" and has been defined as luxury for the masses.[12] Mass-tige brands are considered luxury or premium brands. Their price points fill the gap between the top of the mid-market and the super-premium market that comprises highly select brands. Middle-market consumers in the United States and around the world are trading up to new luxury products and services that deliver higher levels of quality and taste than conventional items. Because such new luxury goods sell for 20 percent to 200 percent more than standard midprice goods, they generate higher profits. They also can sell in much higher volumes than highly selective brands and thus have greater growth potential.

The many examples of repositioning that makes luxury affordable for all[13] include charter aircraft, BMW's Series 3, espresso machines, vintage alcohol, and even dinner at 21 Club. Many fashion-oriented retailers, followed by mass retailers such as Wal-Mart, Carrefour, and Auchan, are playing the game of high class, low price.[14, 15, 16] This tactic is particularly evident in women's and even men's apparel. Wal-Mart is hoping to prove it can reach affluent male consumers by selling Bond St. suits at $2,999.97.[17] Topshop in England became one of the world's hottest retailers by giving its budget fashions an air of exclusivity. Pricey jeans are passé.[18] The Body Shop is repositioning to target the mass-tige segment.[19] The L'Oréal group is doing the same with some of its brands.[20] Target, a major distributor, is accentuating its core strength: affordable chic.[21] Many other companies, ranging from Coach to Karl Lagerfeld, are lamenting the disappearance of free-spending shoppers.[22] More recently, hypermarkets have been extending their creation of in-store universes (of having in-store universes within a store with specific atmosphere and a specific ambience appealing to targeted customers) from cosmetics to apparel. Of course, private labels are part of the game. Merchandising is being fine-tuned to simulate the codes of luxury. The Zara concept (referring to the store Zara's invention of just-in-time fashion concept and delivery) is being extended to hypermarkets.[23]

At the same time, luxury brands are appearing on the Web. Consumers can easily find cheap luxury online. The practice of e-mail alerts is burgeoning—for "special" clients only, of course! Busy female executives can find Valentino dresses online at bargain prices. The value is unbelievable: consumers can book a heavily discounted room in a luxury hotel as unexpected cancellations are flowing in, whatever the reason. Some online Web sites are even organizing auctions of certified luxury products. Consumers can name their own price for Tourneau watches, Hermes and Chanel handbags, and tons of gold jewelry.[24] By luring luxury brands to the Web, some Web sites are helping high-fashion icons move online without going (too far) downscale.[25]

The success of mass-tige is real. Companies offering the irresistible combination of low prices and high quality are capturing the hearts and wallets of consumers in Europe and in the United States, where more than half of the population now shops weekly at mass merchants, both online and off. The market share gains of value-based players are definitely giving their higher-priced rivals cause for alarm.[26] This is much more than a simple shift in value. It is about the shift to high value at an affordable price. The overall ranking of customer satisfaction on sites like Amazon indicates that lower prices have not affected quality at all. In a sector like digital cameras, most brands and models are getting high scores from customers. People rightly perceive that they really are getting more for less. The question is how far can we go? Are there limits to value as a competitive edge and the virtuous circle? The key is to manage expectations well. You must not surpass people's expectations too much and too consistently because your costs have to stay reasonable.

The Two-Way Flow of PPP: Incumbents Down, Newcomers Up

The decline of the purchasing power of incumbents, particularly in Europe and in North America, has become more than an economic fact. It is now a highly sensitive political issue. This socioeconomic phenomenon is not surprising. It is linked to the overall consequences of trading in a flat world, in which not only production is outsourced but also knowledge and even innovation are part of the irresponsible, frenetic pursuit of cost cutting. If some emergent countries are adding to their wealth fairly quickly, the incremental improvements in their lifestyles are dragging down the standard of living in incumbent countries because the worldwide economy is fully connected. The basic physics principle of the communicating vessels applies to the global economy. Twenty years ago, during the development phase of globalization and its related business practices, Noel Goutard, former CEO of Valeo (a car equipment manufacturer) repeatedly hammered into his top executives that globalization is a general impoverishment. He was right. Of course, he was referring to incumbent economies.

In France, for example, inclusion in the European community, combined with the even broader globalization of worldwide markets, has eliminated protectionism. The country and its consumers are currently facing a severe decline in their purchasing power.[27] This is, predictably, creating severe social conflicts. Fierce competition is raging around the world. The sinking PPP (purchase power parity) is not only creating frustration; it is also hard to accept and is forcing people to alter their buying behaviors dramatically. One example is that the allocation of family expenses has changed. Expenses for holidays and other discretionary activities are being slashed. Their relative importance in the family budget is shrinking. There has been a systematic decrease in impulse buying in recent years. In the United States, the data show a sharp drop in consumer credit: in 2009, this drop was three times larger than analysts' estimates (Reuters). Daily amenities—eating out, personal-care products and services, and apparel—tend to suffer. What went up must go down. Conversely, in emerging countries, there is a burgeoning bourgeoisie—the new middle class.[28]

Of course, there are as many definitions of a middle class as there are discussions about the most accurate measures of purchasing power across countries. Regardless, the actual recession may stall middle-class growth but not for long. The incumbent economies are on a slippery slope. The only real question right now is not how to stop this decline; rather, it is whether the reverse (or two-sided) tendencies in purchasing power will stabilize at the equilibrium. It might take years before the PPP among incumbents and emerging countries stabilizes.

According to Maslow's hierarchical theory of human behavior, as soon as the inhabitants of emerging countries have attended to food and security issues, they will presumably start trying to meet "belonging" and "esteem" needs. This shift in the motivations of consumers in emerging economies is already a reality. We can see it in China[29, 30, 31] and India.[32, 33] However, the lackluster performance of Brazil's economy over the past decade is driving consumers toward lower-priced products and services. Purchasing power remains very low.[34] Instead of keeping the focus on the saturated markets in developed countries, the multinationals are naturally gravitating to a huge market opportunity. A critical new battleground is the "good-enough" market segment in China, home of reliable enough products at low enough prices to attract the most affluent of the country's fast-growing cohort of midlevel consumers. Although food is the largest category of spending in China, spending on other categories will increase faster. The new middle class might replace the upper class in relative attractiveness.[35]

For the incumbents, the problem is that their multinationals do not bring home the huge profits they are making abroad, and they don't share monetary value by paying their taxes in their domestic market. Several months after taking office, President Obama began looking into this problem. The total amount of "traveling" profits is estimated at $700 billion (though it is probably higher). The majority of companies in the Global Fortune 500 ranking are U.S. multinationals. They create value (cash), stockpile it, and keep it abroad. American journalists, in search of a large and comprehensive audience, then clamor for protectionism. This gap between economic reality and partisan media claims is paradoxical, but it might be anodyne for the general public.

Perhaps some U.S. business commentators should fight for profit repatriation instead.

Don't forget that the Chinese intend to move from manufacturing commodities to delivering value-added products and services. They are fed up with being isolated as low-value commodity producers. They want to increase the number of Chinese companies in the Global Fortune 500. They know that value creation is the answer because it allows premium pricing. This means the global competitive structure will change even more drastically in the coming years.

Brands Play Musical Chairs: And the Winner Is... Private Labels

If the very large manufacturer brands are still generating billions of dollars in revenues, they are increasingly deriving their profits from emerging countries; they are protecting their margins through radical rationalization of their global product line. They are endeavoring to "massify" their R&D and are increasingly using umbrella branding to rein in marketing costs, even if it clashes with their internal culture (as with P&G). Obviously, they have understood that the sustainability of their margins is as important as their growth. They are trying to withstand what they call "difficult economic conditions."[36]

On the worldwide markets, the quest for high value at a low cost is a tremendous opportunity for the private labels, also called house brands, because they are branded either with the name of the retailer or they share an umbrella name. As retailers have become more powerful and global, they have increasingly cultivated their own brands at the expense of manufacturer brands.[37, 38, and 39] Generics, for example, are making substantial gains in the shelf war. Private labels are shedding their reputation as cheap knockoffs as they expand and challenge name brands.[40] The battle is extremely fierce: whoever owns the brand owns the market. Mass distributors fully understand that distributor branding (banner and private labels combined) is a source of value creation.

When private labels first appeared, many marketing experts proclaimed that they would never gain more than a 20 percent market share. Were they ever wrong. In many sectors, including food products, their market share is well over 20 percent. Not only are retailers playing hardball, but the ongoing commoditization of products and services is an excellent market opportunity for private labels, particularly in developed countries. In Europe, for example, their overall market share was already 23 percent in 2005 (Nielsen: a prestigious market share agency). This continent has the highest penetration in the world, but the growth rate is highest in the emergent countries, at more than 10 percent a year. Penetration rates (that is, sales of generics divided by total sales—in volumes or in dollars) are changing considerably between countries: Germany is an obvious leader, with more than 30 percent, followed closely by France and the United Kingdom.

Some extensions of private labels to a vast range of product categories are quite spectacular, albeit limited: Italian mass distributor Finiper sold its own brand of low-cost SUV for several months. The stock was available in the parking lot, of course! Their continental diffusion was facilitated because their products are carried by specific categories of low-cost retailers. Hard discounters, especially German ones, are using house brands as a competitive edge. Their successful business format, which capitalizes on a real decrease in purchasing power among consumers in different countries, is boosting their private labels considerably.[41] The average price gap between private labels and manufacturer brands is about 30 percent. It has recently increased. Evidently, this gap varies between countries, depending upon both the legislation and the competitiveness of the price-quality relationship. For example, the value associated with Tesco (a famous British international and general merchandising retail chain) is not merely "good and less expensive." This product line is perceived as "the best," with very high customer appeal; it is now a national reference for high quality at a fair price.[42] Consequently, the price gap of Tesco is only 10 percent.

There are three main factors behind the spectacular rise of private labels. First, they are no longer associated with low perceived quality. At the same time, consumers are less inclined to take the "virtues" of manufacturer brands for granted.[43] The second reason, related to the first, is that private labels have a strong appeal among younger consumers.[44] Third, their relatively lower prices are a perfect fit with the idea of reducing costs to keep pace with shrinking consumption budgets and new lifestyles (people unwilling to waste their time shopping visit major chains where a large assortment of house brands is available). Massive buying of lower-priced private-label brands can effectively combat reduced purchasing power. It's the perfect solution to the major problem many consumers from developed economies are suddenly facing, but one to which their counterparts in emerging countries have long since adapted.

At the same time, loyalty to this category of brands is increasing. The previous chapter argued that absolute loyalty to manufacturer brands is declining because of the infinite choice and increased perceived parity. Conversely, loyalty to private labels is increasing, especially among young people. The private labels are perceived to be as efficient as those of manufacturers; consumers' readiness to buy is increasing, and the products' range is expanding steadily. Private labels have spread from the food sector to beauty products, office furniture, electronics, building hardware, and apparel. The possibilities are endless. Major distributors are ready to go even further; they are tracking the evolving needs of worldwide consumers and responding to them perfectly. Clearly, marketing expertise is not exclusive to the big manufacturers. As for marketing strategy, it is time to acknowledge that the capacities of mass distributors are often superior to those of many large manufacturers. Mass distributors tend to be much more proactive than manufacturers. They are always one step ahead in managing a new trend, be it an opportunity or a threat to their business. When the Internet first took off, mass distributors quickly realized it might be a source of disintermediation and consequently a threat. To prevent manufacturers from cultivating this avenue, they acted quickly to launch their own Web sites first and rapidly developed e-commerce activities.

Vertical conflicts between manufacturers and mass distributors are intense, even if officially they speak about "win-win" partnerships. The trade negotiations are ruthless, and the ambiance is complex. But of course, margins are at center stage once again. Hypercompetition is putting a lot of pressure on retail or list prices. Margin loss has to be regained one way or another. It is natural to want to pass the burden to a business "partner," transforming the theoretical approach from "win-win" to "win-lose." The game of markups and markdowns is being played mercilessly.[45] Professional practices are not always fair, and some major distributors do not hesitate to de-reference manufacturer brands (that is, these distributors can decide to get rid of one brand and to get it out of the shelves of their stores) if they do not meet their commercial and financial requirements, arguing that they are putting the end consumers first and trying to protect their purchasing power. They can be compared to modern-day Robin Hoods!

The Power of Organizing Without Organizations: Online Networking

"My son has a 'friend' in Australia.... But he doesn't even know his neighbor.... Can you believe it?" So said a concerned, disheartened father in the province of Quebec (known for its tight-knit communities, especially during the winter!).

This reaction is understandable; it speaks for itself. Many people are completely disconnected from the real world in general and from particular concrete activities such as traveling, visiting museums, participating in outdoor events, and even shopping! They live online. If they travel abroad, they eagerly look for an Internet connection or will stay in their hotel room to read their e-mail or check what their "friends" are doing on a day-to-day basis by connecting to Facebook, MySpace, YouTube, or Twitter.

From a business perspective, the issue is not only to understand online shoppers and their behaviors, which vary strongly among segments and among countries.[46] The main challenge is to harness the power of online social communities. Companies are struggling with a new megatrend that is unstoppable, global, and affecting their commercial activities dramatically: the power of organizing without organizations.[47] This sweeping, tsunami-force trend has become a real obsession in the business world. Executives are trying hard to regain control and tap into online communities of "friends," but the counterreactions to their attempts are strong and unpredictable at times. Clear thinking is required because many potential downsizings or backlashes make this game dangerous and complex. Facebook CEO Mark Zuckerberg, who reportedly said, "There is no opting out of advertising," learned this lesson the hard way after he faced a strong revolt among his users when he tried to launch a new system known as Facebook Ads, which allowed companies to create their own profile pages. It was perceived by users as an intrusion in their online private life. They were not willing to give companies access to all of their final consumption choices, nor would they let the choices be broadcast to their own community of friends without their permission.

An online social community is a buzz machine that can work both ways: on the positive side, it creates viral marketing at a low cost; the downside is that it can trigger spontaneous brand destruction. Despite the business risks, the three-way battle among the multinationals and the members and hubs of the communities is raging.

Companies are obsessed with online communities. There are three major motivations behind their eagerness to navigate this new dynamic and dangerous landscape of consumer vigilantes.[48] Number one: companies are losing control over their customers. They cannot manipulate them as easily as they did before. Naturally, they find this hard to accept. The Internet allows total transparency: dissatisfied customers can easily express their frustrations or anger online. A disgruntled airline passenger spawned a national movement with her blog. Complaints about Dell computers' customer service were posted on the Web.[49, 50] There are blogs dedicated to consumer complaints. Negative buzz marketing is definitely something to worry about. On Web sites such as Tripadvisor, people are providing detailed feedback about the hotels they visited. The gap between the business world and the customer world is shrinking. People are better informed than ever and are spreading information worldwide.

Second, many consumers are disengaged from real life in general and commercial life in particular. Overall, people are less engaged in consumption than they were before. The time they spend online is devoted much more to social activities such as chatting or dating than to discussions specifically about consumption. There is an important distinction between encouraging customer engagement and preventing customer disengagement.[51] Reengaging people in business and commercial activities is crucial, but it is harder than it seems: marketers are out of control. Companies must find new ways to encourage consumers to participate and fully collaborate in their business life. Two areas of participation are particularly hot: advertising management and product innovation. Preventing customer disengagement is another story. Not only are different techniques required, but their chances of success are lower.

The third and last factor follows from the previous one. Online communities tend to be very business-wary and vigilant. They object to corporate intrusion, for obvious commercial purposes, in their online private life. They savor their newly acquired freedom and are determined to broaden it.

The Commoditization Phenomenon: Are Consumers Affected?

To conclude this chapter, bear in mind that commoditization does not affect the supply side only. It is increasingly a two-faceted economic phenomenon. People, as consumers, are commoditized, too. They spend a lot of their time connected to others and are creating a new social community. The more they connect, the more they weaken their general knowledge. Most users exchange a lot more information on trivial topics than on science, economics, and mathematics.

The Web is a democratizing force. It educates everyone on the pros and cons of every product or service. "Educated" people do not react the same way as others to the traditional art of manipulation that most marketing agencies tended to employ in their mass campaigns. It is making them angry and potentially defensive. The new generation of young adults has grown up with interactive technologies and is not set in its mass-media-usage habits. As a result, it is not intimidated by technology and is much harder to control.

There are two important questions to consider. The first is this: Are you expecting your customers to respond the way they used to? Many marketers still are, and that is the problem. But there is another issue here. We have begun to funnel cultural, political, and community activities through online connections. Consumers are probably not adopting products for what they really are but as expressions of their identities. We are building an online community of individualists.

We can then ask this: Is this good news or bad news? Well, it is good news when network-literate young people freely and willingly co-opt brands instead of being corrupted by commercials. It is bad news when they no longer fully appreciate what they are really buying. They have no idea about the intrinsic characteristics that make some products or services unique. Their lack of general culture is not reinforcing the so-called secret dialogue between what they buy and who they are.[52]

The commoditization of products might be driven mainly by globalization, resulting in an infinite choice of ostensibly similar products and services. In contrast, the commoditization of consumers undoubtedly results mainly from overengagement in online activities. When there is a lack of real culture, everything turns into a theme park. Some online sites can even be accused of hampering users' education.

Naturally, companies will try to spoon-feed their potential clientele. Why should they offer complex lines when consumers cannot even understand and appreciate complexity? The wine industry provides a dismaying example. People should choose a bottle because of its provenance, not because of the color of the sticker and the attractiveness of the logo. Cognacs have become white because they look more attractive and "cooler," that is, more like vodka. Of course, it is better to sell a white cognac than nothing. Traditional brown-colored aged cognacs have lost ground to white cognacs, which lack a history but have strong perceived value among heavy drinkers at an affordable price. The movie *Mondovino* clearly depicts the recent seismic shifts in the global wine industry.[53]

The final key question to ponder is this: How can a company cope with such radical changes? I will let you make up your mind while we probe the customer value creation process. At least I dared to ask the question.

PART 2

Defining Business Prerequisites (and Ideals) Prior to Action

CHAPTER 3

The Value-for-Money Business Perspective

> For many years, rightly or wrongly, it was assumed that the sole objective of a company listed on the stock market was to generate maximum, ever growing value for the shareholders. This narrow concept of the role of a company has brought us to a dead end. I see this as one of the major lessons of the crisis.
>
> —Franck Riboud, CEO, Danone[1]

Finally! There is a breath of fresh air in the international business and finance world. Even the CEO of Danone has publicly admitted that the frenetic search for profit maximization is not sustainable. The downturn is so harsh that it has led many chief executives and governments to seriously discuss intensified regulation of the liberal approach and the urgent need for a new economic order. The resulting idea—a new economic "generation"—is a hot topic. The exact meaning of this new idea, however, is far from clear. How far should governments go in their effort to regulate business practices? The G20 meeting in London in March 2009 is unanimously considered a historical day. For the first time, countries around the world signed a resolution to regulate finance and international trade and invested heavily in the effort to fight poverty. Granted, there is still room for improvement. More concrete and radical political decisions are needed. Patience is also essential, despite the urgency of restoring order to the economy and business practices. The global economic crisis is so real that lessons must be learned and major corrective actions must be taken. Inertia is not an option. It would be extremely dangerous and might generate a social explosion on the global scale. Up to now, public reactions have arisen only in certain countries, Italy and France, for example. If the exasperation of populations around the world increases even more, things might turn ugly because too many people are directly and severely affected, and they are well aware that bad business practices are a major cause of their woes. For example, banks (and their bonuses) are under close scrutiny, not only in Europe, but also in the United States. People around the world expect corrective measures to be taken immediately. Trust in business is dissolving. Since the recession, it has plummeted. The Elder Trust Barometer (an annual global opinion leader study) found that 62 percent of adults in 20 countries trusted corporations less in December 2008 than they had a year earlier. This is a dangerous trend business executives have to take very seriously.[2] Without trust in business, there cannot be a strong, thriving economy.

Countries and companies must manage the equilibriums within a twofold process: the cultivation of economic development and social wealth. In organizational management, the links and interests of all partners, from employees to suppliers, together with local territories where operations occur, must be simultaneously taken into account. All of these actors participate in the process of value creation or, more precisely, wealth production. Within this extended framework, some actors will probably feel as if they are being ignored. Their willingness to be heard by companies (and indirectly by government as it regulates business practices) is greater than ever.

Companies must adopt an ecosystem perspective. This perspective should not be limited to environmental issues such as climate. Actively taking global warming into account, though extremely important, is insufficient in itself. There are many other critical issues at stake, such as poverty, ecology, and health. The scope of corporate social responsibility should also be extended to solidarity with all the stakeholders. In other words, a company must generate value for its shareholders because without their investment, there is no economy. A company must also generate value and wealth for the other actors, particularly the employees and the customers. This is the only way for companies to acquire social utility.

These newly rekindled debates are compulsory for three main reasons. The first is that the recession of 2008 (and the years to come) has generated severe social events. It has also brought to light too many unscrupulous business practices that must be addressed and eliminated. Second, it is impossible to manage a company effectively without considering the human and social issues. This is the only difference between good and bad executives, between companies that are efficient and responsible and those that are not. The third and last reason is that the two previous issues are closely related on a specific point: value creation and distribution. Both value-related actions are the common denominator of business decisions. They also directly shape the way companies address commoditization and underlie the current recession. Creating customer value is a major corporate goal among companies willing to reverse the tide of commoditization constructively. Cutting costs systematically without sound strategic considerations signals corporate irresponsibility and a reactive and destructive mode to fighting commoditization.

This type of challenging discussion on companies' attitudes, constructive or negative, must occur now. Clear positions should be defined prior to any action or strategic recommendation. This prerequisite is universal and should have the force of law. Prior to any further discussion of corrective actions and strategic recommendations intended to reverse the tide of commoditization, this chapter presents my specific vision of business from a value creation perspective.

The Contentious Polemic: New Ideals or New Business Models?

The question is not whether a company should generate a profit or not. Executives who forget that a satisfactory profit is the main criterion of success and of sustainability would drive their company to its ruin. The important questions are how to build long-term profitability and how to consider the constraints and interests of the stakeholders involved. In a nutshell, the goal is to manage complex equilibriums and unavoidable contradictions between efficiency and humanity, competitiveness and protectionism, the short and long term, individual interests and collective well-being, and so on.

The debate on these issues is raging. Reactions have been highly emotional. People are angrier than ever and showing it. This is not surprising. The fact that this debate is truly under way is a positive sign. The debate in itself is not new, but it has been exacerbated by the severity of the public outcry. The downturn is so dire and its present and future consequences so unpredictable that business experts have called it the "zombie economy." The business turbulence is so intense that it has ignited a fierce debate on how ideals should guide the reinvention of business models. Such a debate is a manifesto for smart growth, fair business, more ethics in business practices, and, of course, the implementation of regulation in all economic sectors, in particular the finance world. Within this strict perspective, boardrooms must rethink their priorities when redesigning models. Lower costs, greater efficiency, and choosing the most profitable customers and revenue streams should not be their only goals. Some people argue that business models aren't today's fundamental economic challenge.[3] Business model innovation is exactly the wrong thing to focus on, they contend. Creating something valuable in the first place is the right thing. It is by rediscovering how to make products that are not toxic junk that business will get out of the mess we have been left in by lame, evil, brain-dead twentieth-century thinking. For companies that make valuable products, there are a plethora of business models to choose from. Their conclusion is clearly and strongly stated: no amount of business model innovation can save us from implosion.

This strong position is intellectually attractive and is probably a valid business philosophy. It resembles a socialist precept in political terms. I believe that instead of rejecting the reinvention of business models outright, it is better to find a middle ground. The quest for ideals cannot be dissociated from the invention, development, and sustainability of business models. When ideas become tainted with a political brush, receptivity to the best ideas suffers.

At the beginning of this chapter, I quoted Mr. Riboud and lauded his quest for a more social perspective to the management of large companies, including Danone. Although his ideas have been hotly debated by the French media, paradoxically, his views have been systematically rejected by business journalists belonging to the so-called political "left." At first glance, increasing the focus on social issues is clearly a left-wing political idea that should be wholly supported by socialists because it echoes their staunch claims. Left-wing journalists, however, rejected the views because the quest for a more social perspective was expressed by a top executive, commonly called a *patron* (boss) in France. Now all the economic actors are at a loss, and regulatory proposals are stagnating.

Repeating robotically that the customer is the boss without acting accordingly is worthless. If you really believe in delighting your customers, and if you are ready to invest both your time and your money to do it, you will design your business accordingly. You will then provide your customers with a strong solution or experience and be rewarded for acting positively. Lamenting that "monetizing-plus" business models equals the building of a zombie economy is not the solution. It is a catchy claim, but it is misleading. A much better approach would stress putting ideals first, followed by the resulting creation, invention, or reinvention (it hardly matters) of a business model that incorporates the ideals stated above. Most importantly, the business model must deliver value to the customer first. Profitability will be the final reward (not a goal). Before that, you will experience strong performance in customer satisfaction, followed by an increase in your market share and resulting organic growth. As an entrepreneur, you must invest in your business and assume the inherent risks. Do not expect customers to come to you and buy more of your products or services in order to support your development. It's not their job. The better you fulfill your customers' needs, the more they will buy your products or services—not the reverse. Too many entrepreneurs have asked the customers to boost their support to help them improve their quality of service and help their business survive. For example, the owner of a local newspaper asked the general public to read his paper more so he could hire better journalists. This request is preposterous. You must earn your customers first! Do not try to reverse the rule of business practice, which is, by definition, risky. If you do not want to take on risk, stay out of the business world. You are not an entrepreneur.

To conclude on the key role of ideals, which should be integrated in the development, management, and sustainability of business models, consider the concept of the "performance trinity," made up of "leadership and management," "cultures and values," and "vision and strategy."[4] The third of those three elements is "hard" (or concrete) but is the easiest to formulate. The real challenge lies in tackling the two "soft" elements. If positively managed, both foster value for customers, employees, partners, and investors.

The Provocative Question: Did You Say Value?

At the end of 2008, just after the recession officially began, a well-known finance guru gave a formal speech to several hundred businesspeople in Montreal. Using vivid argumentation to endorse the current finance world, coupled with an upbeat statement on the predictable rebound of the United States and supported by an impressive in-depth analysis of the history of the Dow Jones, the speaker urged the audience to buy more stocks immediately. By acting now (i.e., the day of his speech), they would make a lot of money and refuel the (U.S.) economy. He did not question why we were all mired in this economic mess. He did not address the massive amounts of money individuals lost in their retirement plans, most often without being entitled to redeem them. This is because the plans are managed according to rules. Such rules have been developed to somewhat protect the financial institutions. For example if you want to redeem your retirement plan sooner, you will have to pay strong penalties. He added that things will certainly return to normal soon. He received a standing ovation. The audience was totally reassured. Let us hope that few people followed his strong recommendation to buy stocks at that time to offset their losses because obviously things have worsened since then. Why are some business executives so naïve?

Adopting a similarly radical approach, many experts are giving speeches and writing books and articles to promote their own perspectives and recipes to create "value." Too many of them are making strong assumptions that are later proven to be false or unreliable, as is their rhetoric. A small number of them admit they are wrong and slink off in shame. More often than not, though, they simply write another best seller backed with new certainties, which are equally questionable. This stance is admittedly cynical, but I feel it is the truth. There is one category of business books that can be trusted. These are characterized by a rigorous inductive research approach. They do not present personal and highly subjective assertions on business practices that they then try earnestly to justify. They usually select a representative sample of companies. Then they benchmark the best and worst practices and companies. They integrate lessons from the field to build a reliable theory or business model. Businesspeople would be best served by reading only this type of sound publication. You will not waste your money on books of dubious quality, which might even be extremely dangerous because of the false strategic recommendations they contain. It is easy, as a so-called expert, to say you are sorry if the implementation of your recommendations in companies has caused serious collateral damage, particularly socially. It is even worse to say nothing and simply churn out another book following the same pattern. To avoid a halo effect of these remarks on both the content of the following paragraphs and on the references below, I will not discuss such irresponsible practices again.

When it comes to value creation, the majority of business experts, individuals, and consulting companies focus on creating value for the shareholders. They promote a strict financial-only perspective, coupled with the goal of making profits easily and quickly. Financial analyses, backed by statistical calculations, generally dominate business publications.[5,6] Managing from an investor perspective is viewed by many business executives as a supreme guide to decision making in both good times and bad. Their basic underlying assumption is that investors are always anticipating that a company's prospects will brighten.[7] The stock exchange then becomes a vast information system from a marketing perspective! This is fine, but what about the short-term investment behaviors that might hamper the internal, long-term equilibrium of a company? Instead of looking at shareholder value as the only point of reference, perhaps businesspeople should perceive it merely as a grading system. Whether it is a reliable one is another story. Remember the number of financial institutions rated triple A the day before they crashed. How could a financial advisor justify investment recommendations to clients based on such unreliable standards?

Another provocative book on the subject of value creation deals with the granularity of growth. The question is how to identify the sources of growth and enduring company performance.[8] Once again, the overall growth of a set of large U.S. companies is linked to the total shareholder return. The idea is to disaggregate your company's performance from one global market to another one so that you understand how your business "cylinders" fire at the segment and subsegment level. Undoubtedly, this analysis provides a very useful macroanalytic way to understand your performance on a global and local basis. However, it does not explain performance (good or poor) in worldwide segments or subsegments; it only describes it, though this is certainly the first step to take in the right direction.

Too often, the studies of growth and value creation systematically downplay or rule out any perspective other than financial returns in general and returns to shareholders in particular. They have little regard for customer value creation. They simply ignore it. Of course, creating value for the employees and business partners such as suppliers is also out of the question or is only a minor consideration. The resulting consequences in the business world are bizarre. For instance, Costco, a mass distributor, experienced an instantaneous plunge in its stock value a few hours after announcing very positive financial results. Why? Most of their sales ratios were much better than Wal-Mart's. Both employee and customer satisfaction were higher, and the social cost per employee was lower. Greedy shareholders were expecting even more! They asked for unjustifiable layoffs in an effort to improve the overall profitability of the company and the associated returns. The CEO refused. He should have been congratulated for this courageous stance. Most of the time, a counterreaction to the power of shareholders might result in pressure on the CEO to resign. Too often, greedy investors call the shots.

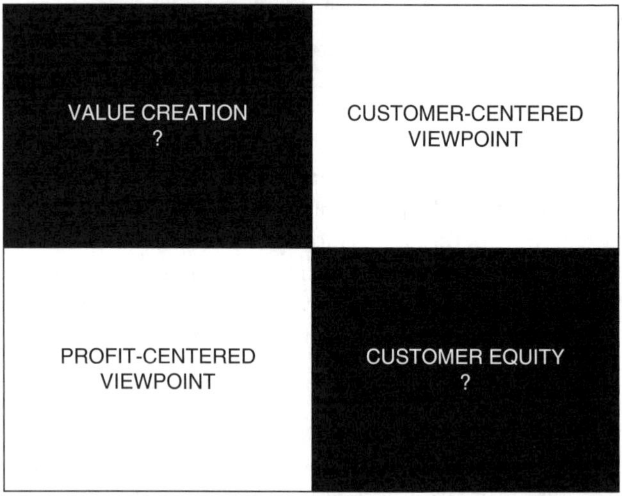

Figure 3.1 The trade-off on value.

For many companies, margins have been squeezed by commoditization. The result is extreme trade-offs between the short and the long term, between customer and shareholder value, and between the long-term sustainability of the company and the short-term necessity to pay for the diktat of shareholders (see figure 3.1).

Consequently, the word "value" has been completely stripped of its deepest connotation (see figure 3.2). "Profit building or wealth creation" should replace "profit making." Value-based management (VBM) and customer value management (CVM) should not be confused with customer value creation (CVC). Within a VBM approach, the unit of analysis is the business unit. The objective is to make the business unit as profitable as possible. CVM is based on value segmentation, which means the main idea is to identify the most profitable customers, under the Pareto Principle (the 80/20 rule) (that is to say, 20 per cent of the customers contribute to 80 percent of the business' sales volume and total profits). Only CVC can be viewed as a real customer-centered approach because it entails generating customer satisfaction first. The misunderstanding of the business concepts and the resulting misleading business paradigms are much more than a simple question of semantics. The real problem is the primacy in business practice of short-term over long-term considerations. Radical

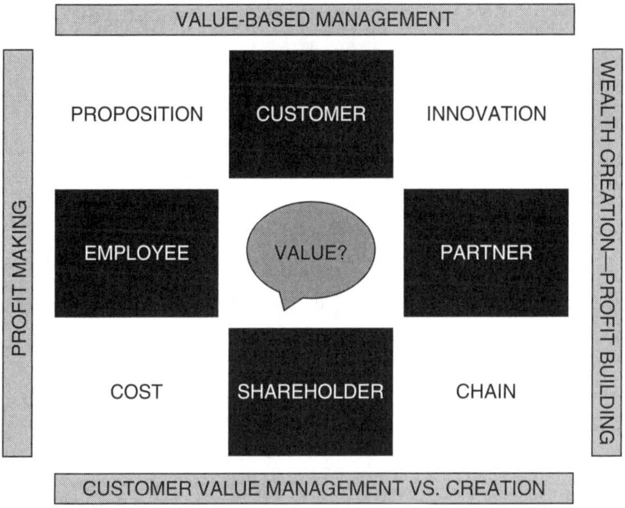

Figure 3.2 The semantic distortions on the meaning of value.

cost cutting and speedy profit making are destructively undermining fair value creation in general and long-term customer value creation in particular. From a cynical standpoint, such wrong fundamentals are the main source of what might be called creative self-destruction, which is accelerating the decline of business. It is the opposite of what should be done during a difficult period, particularly a severe recession.[9] Intellectually, such destructive attitudes and behaviors are difficult to understand—and to accept—because looking at customer value as the next source of competitive advantage was addressed as early as 1997.[10] The practical relation of the concepts (of management and competitiveness) to customer value creation, even in business markets, has long been explained.[11] Many articles and chapters have been published to help busy managers absorb and apply such concepts, especially as they grow their businesses.[12] The ways suppliers can figure out exactly what their offerings are worth by creating and using customer value models have also been illustrated.[13] All of these experts focus on creating a competitive advantage to fight commoditization, yet business executives are still reluctant to apply these concepts. I will not add to the debate about why because it is not germane to the practical approach of this book. The social sciences could provide a better answer.

Consider CRM (customer relationship management). There are as many definitions of this business process as there are authors. Yet they all have one point in common: the idea that an individualized relationship with the customer, on a one-to-one basis, should be grounded in sharing the "mutual benefits" between the company and the customer. CRM should allow a company to be rewarded (increasing sales and profits) by developing the quality of the client's experience.[14] This two-sided business relationship is called a "win-win" approach. If you look more closely at the basic concepts associated with CRM, however, you might notice some biases. One example is the value segmentation paradigm. Instead of brand differentiation, the idea of this is to cross the border between supply and demand, to focus on customer differentiation. Some customers (a minority) are extremely profitable. Others are draining money out of the company. The second group tends to be much larger than the first. What should companies do about the second group? Financial institutions such as ING North America decided to fire their least profitable clients!

This radical approach has been explained by the CEO of ING Direct, Arkadi Kuhlmann: " 'We fire our customers' is a colorful way of putting it," said ING Direct's Kuhlmann, "While the banking business says the customer is always right, we're online guys and you can only do business with us in a certain way."[15]

Conversely, a handful of banks—Wells Fargo, for one—try to understand why some of their customers are not profitable and are working hard to make them change their behavior. The difference is that in the first example (ING), the unprofitable customers are guilty. In the second one (Wells Fargo), the bank admits its own guilt to the public and to its employees.

It is not surprising that many implementations of CRM processes in companies failed. As a result, this business process has been seriously questioned. CRM does work, as long as it is done well.[16] It is very effective if a company is not using its database only to control its customers, without sharing some of the benefits of its technology with them. Recently, a growing number of implementations of CRM processes have been successful because of a better understanding of CRM requirements, translated by a focus on the sharing of benefits between companies and their customers. Let's hope the severity of the downturn will not cancel out the recent advancements of CRM by reviving the negative effects of compulsive cost control. Although the downturn should theoretically reinforce the role of the customer in the

CRM process, the opposite may occur. Creative self-destruction might resurge.

The Biggest Bang for the Buck: Growth and Stock Value

Innovation capacity is believed to create and sustain successful growth. The growth paradox is that at best, one company in ten is able to sustain profitable growth. Why? Surprisingly, it's not because of the lack of great ideas or capable managers or because customers are too fickle or innovation too unpredictable. Innovation fails because organizations unwittingly strip the disruptive potential from new ideas before they ever see the light of day.[17]

The study of innovation and its business impact has produced another startling finding: in the configuration of business models driving best growth and stock value, the best results come (once again) from customer-centered viewpoints rather than profit-oriented viewpoints.[18]

The *BusinessWeek* Innovation Index tracked 25 corporations known for their forward-thinking products, processes, consumer experience, or business models. Cross-tabbing the average annual growth in 2004–2007 (the horizontal axis) by the average stock returns of the same period of time (vertical axis) showed that the companies with innovative business models tend to have the best scores on both axes. *BusinessWeek* pointed out that the creation of hip devices like the iPhone may not be the most profitable form of innovation. In fact, an innovative business model should be defined as the resulting combination of innovative products, innovative customer experience, and innovative processes. The relative weight of each type of innovation as a contribution to the final configuration of an innovative business model is harder to pinpoint, as is the internal synergy between the different types of innovation following an additive or multiplicative interaction.

Two major ideas follow from this analysis. First, business innovation, as a driver of value creation, is wholly dependent on the customers' perception. Perception is reality. This means that the creative and positive qualities of a commercial offering are not defined in the company. All the same, the customers' positive reactions may come from several dimensions of this offering. Some very original (and very rare) cult brands create their own positive perceptions, whereas other more commonplace brands of products stand out because of the innovative service they feature. The service experience counts here more than the product experience as such. Lastly, the positive perception of a commercial offering can come from its exceptional accessibility. In this case, innovation involves the business process; often highly efficient logistics make a very noticeable difference.

The second major idea is that innovation resulting from the highly innovative nature of the business model far exceeds all the other more partial forms of innovation in terms of commercial efficiency. To the customers, it represents a complete business solution, from end to end: the offering combines an optimal product, service, and accessibility. It thus has a much stronger impact on growth and return on equity. This assertion, which advocates an integrated vision of different sources of innovation, is very pertinent to the discussion in chapter 4 on the reinvention of business models. It explains why the business model must be a collage of all the company functions, with the customer value proposition at its center. Emphasis will not be placed on a single function; they must all be considered. This is one of the central ideas of this book.

The Optimal Approach: Spotlighting Value-for-Money

The economic value of a good or service has puzzled economists since the discipline arose. Value-for-money is defined as an audit that judges the quality of provision, processes, or outcomes against the monetary cost of making the provision, undertaking the process, or achieving the outcomes.[19] From a business perspective, value-for-money (VFM) is a term used to assess whether an organization has obtained the maximum benefit from the goods and services it acquires and provides based on the resources available. Notably, the perspective is from the supply side only.

Shifting the perspective to the demand side, or the customer perspective, can be very illuminating. Reframing VFM in a context of tough economic times will help readers understand why and how some companies have outperformed rivals to become market leaders through value-for-money strategies.

In a challenging article, Williamson and Zeng explained that a few bright companies have enabled recession-hit consumers to economize (do less and spend less, become more efficient (do the same for less), or become more effective (do more but spend no more).[20] To implement such strategies, companies must go beyond refining cost-cutting capabilities and develop expertise in cost innovation. That may not be good news for many U.S., European, and Japanese corporations because multinationals from emerging markets, which have long experience with value-conscious customers, have already acquired cost-innovation capabilities that are unlocking mass markets in both developing and developed countries. In response, experts argue, Western companies should turn to developing countries for vital lessons in lowering the cost of building brands and developing and manufacturing products. They conclude that multinationals that fail to learn from emerging rivals are unlikely to weather the recession.

Some companies are in deeper trouble. Not only are they ignoring vital lessons from emerging countries, but they do not understand that the management of a company should simultaneously consider both the top and the bottom of a margin. Pushing the bottom of the margin (the cost) as low they can is these companies' only objective (see figure 3.3).

As mentioned, many executives are obsessed with cutting costs. They are determined to push the margin as low as they can. They say they expect to create value, which translates into protecting the

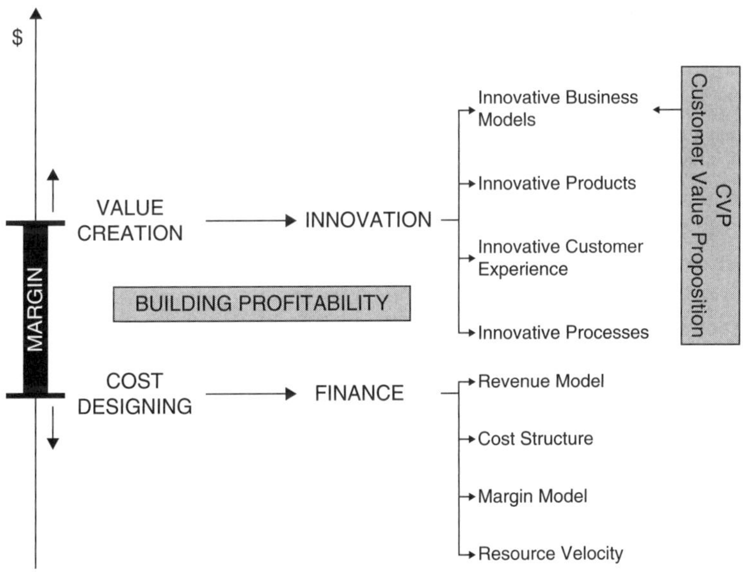

Figure 3.3 The margin-oriented perspective of a company.

profitability of their companies "at all costs." They see every investment as an expense. They are not suffering from "marketing myopia"[21] but from an even more serious disease. They reject all marketing considerations outright. For example, they do not understand that skimping on customer service is a common and sometimes costly response to tough economic times. They are unable to grasp that companies can maintain quality and save money at the same time.[22] Pushing up the top of the margin by creating value for the customer is not in their mindset. Their key words are restructuring plans, social plans and layoffs, growth by acquisitions (of similar companies, also ailing), and so on. By acting in this negative way, they do not create any added value. Many accelerate the speed of their decline. They focus on the cosmetic makeup of quarterly results to prolong, in the very short term, the survival of their jobs, whatever the consequences on the entire organization. Most of them no longer truly believe in the quintessence of their mission. They are fighting for survival, which might trigger generalized panic. Everything then collapses, and employees with drawn faces are shown on television carting off office furniture and files in boxes. Final consumers, especially account holders at defunct financial institutions, are hit even harder: they sometimes lose everything (their houses, their savings, their pensions, etc.).

Customer value creation is much more important than cost cutting. It should be underpinned mainly by innovation that improves the perception of quality by the final customer. For example, innovating in logistics (as a business process) should not only enhance your efficiency and reduce your costs, but it must have a final impact on the customer experience, such as easier access to products and services. Too many executives are not taking the customer into consideration. They are irresponsible and do not deserve to manage a company. This strong position will be revisited in the conclusion. It bears repeating. In fact, the entire business community needs to get the message. Now evidence suggests that shareholders actually do better when firms put the customer first. It is time to make the shift to a new era: customer-driven capitalism.[23]

The Increasing Focus on Positioning and Its Resulting Implementation

The primary goal of an organization should be to leverage results and process quality over costs. This is achieved through a focused, internally consistent operating strategy comprising policies, procedures, organization, controls, incentives, and an organization culture designed to do just that.[24]

The starting point is clear positioning, and the outcome is proper management of customer expectations, especially if a company's values and mission statement are clearly explained and understood by all its partners and in particular by its customers and employees. Your positioning defines the limits of your competences and the boundaries of your implementation and execution.

Once the objective of a business model is well established, the next priority should be making the output attractive to the customer. The focus should be extended to execution, namely implementation and practical feasibility. The last concern is profitability (the bottom line) (see figure 3.4).

During the "dot-com" era in the late 1990s, too many businesspeople, innovators, and investors were focusing on attractiveness. Money was flowing in. The problem, which posed a high risk, was that funding was coming from the stock market, not the market. In March 2000, the tech bubble burst, causing the spectacular crash of the technology-heavy NASDAQ. The pendulum then swung in the opposite direction. People started to focus only on the bottom line. Ideally, a more rational balance between customer attractiveness and the bottom line will be

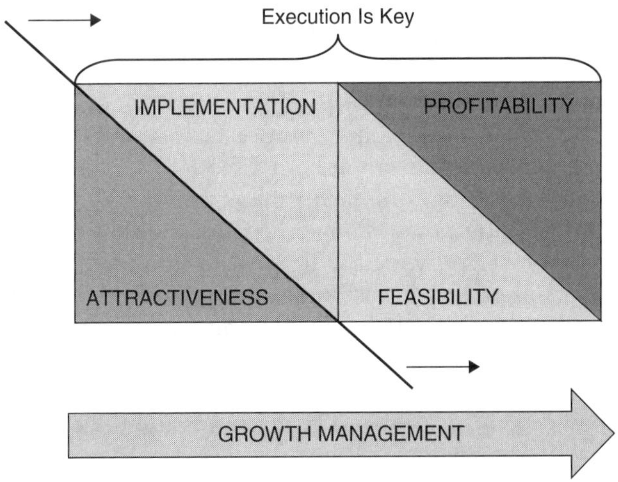

Figure 3.4 A complete perspective of a business model.

struck soon. As often happens, however, we went from one extreme to the other. History is constantly repeating itself, and few really learn from the past.

It is very important to manage expectations well. A low-cost airline must not behave like a regular airline. Granted, some attributes of the business are important for the customer. Planes must be in perfect condition. Pilots should be well trained. Other factors, such as seat selection, are not essential. Offering champagne is out of the question, as this is not part of the business. The airline's customers know very well that they will not drink champagne during the flight. There is no need to surpass their expectations on attributes they do not even consider. Excess perfectionism can be counterproductive in this case.

Here is another telling example. The commoditization of markets has created the perfect environment for the rise of hard-discount stores. This trend is particularly apparent in Europe, where the market share of hard discounters is increasing. A large majority of European customers now visit those no-frills food stores. Germany and even France are leading the pack. The traditional business model of hypermarkets such as Carrefour is under heavy attack. Only Tesco, a unique British chain, is managing to keep the hard discounters at bay: as the CRM champion, they overtly share benefits with their customers, building their loyalty to the banner. They exceed the average client's expectations, but they do not manage their stores the way hard discounters do. In 2009, the growth rate of hard discounters suddenly started to level off. Distribution experts deduced that the hard-discount model was becoming more and more like a soft-discount one.[25] Only one banner was sticking to the original no-frills configuration and was escaping the slowdown: Aldi. The explanation is quite obvious: customers are not expecting fancy merchandising, nice facing, and well-organized shelves in a hard-discount store. If hard discounters improve the assortments, the product ranges in each category, and the overall in-store presentation overnight, they change the rules and the codes. Not only will their costs increase, which will translate into higher retail prices, but they will unsettle their customers, who associate low prices with no frills. To summarize, successful hard discounters should leave the setup alone. All the customers expect from them is to deliver quality products at a very low cost. If they provide more, they will surpass the overall expected performance of the stores and the customer value perception will become foggy. It is as simple as that. Trying to do more would simply undermine the uniqueness of the business model.

Efficiency-Driven Execution: Collaboration and Synergies

Traditionally, the notion of value has been associated with a chain. Value chain analysis is a concept in business management that was first described and popularized by Michael Porter.[26] A value chain is a sequence of activities. Products pass through all activities of the chain in order, and at each activity the product gains value. The chain of activities gives the products more added value than the sum of added value of all activities. It is important not to confuse the concept of the value chain with the costs occurring throughout the activities. A diamond cutter is a fine example of the difference. The cutting activity may have a low cost, but it adds much of the value to the end product because a rough diamond is significantly less valuable than a cut diamond.

The problem with the value chain is that there is a natural tendency to see any business model from a silo perspective. Instead, you need to open your business horizons by participating in value webs. Value is thus built by a network of economic actors creating and participating in your value creation as part of an ecosystem. Dynamic linkage is created with suppliers, distributors, customers, and even competitors. To succeed, your organizational structure must be conceived as a molecular structure, in which many components revolve around your core activity: the pressure of standardization, convergence, and hyper-competition drives "componentization."[27]

In terms of execution and costs, collaboration and synergies between different economic partners drive performance strongly and create more added value for the customer. Here are some revealing examples. In the fishing industry, integration plays a key role. A fishing boat full of tuna can connect via satellite to a broker, allowing negotiation of the catch price prior to the boat's arrival in the harbor. The final result is the delivery of fresher sushi at a lower cost to the final consumer.

Further, revision of BMPs (business management processes) is much more important than integration. Dell used to buy the LCD screen for their computers from Sony. The visible brand is Dell. The screens are delivered direct to UPS. The final packing of the computer and the screen is managed at UPS warehouses. The final delivery is made by UPS in Dell's name. The final buyer has no idea that both Sony and UPS are directly involved in the assembly of the final product (the computer, the screen, and the packaging). Sony is selling more LCD screens at the expense of losing brand equity. Dell recognizes a lack of

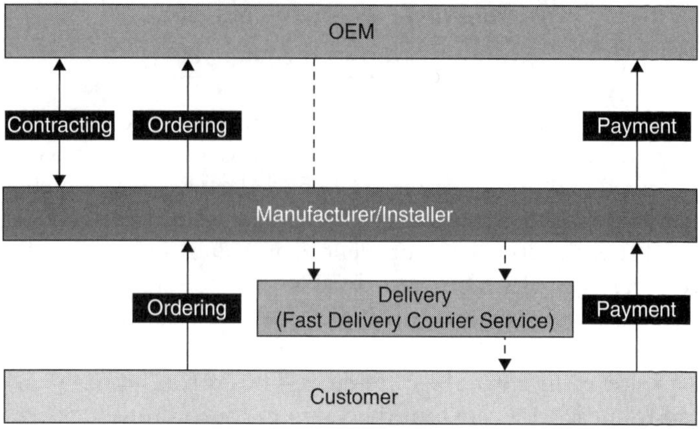

Figure 3.5 Revision rather than integration of BMPs is crucial.

expertise in packaging and delivery. UPS could redefine its business model and escape the current situation of highly commoditized delivery of mail only as a private carrier (see figure 3.5).

Opening business territories in core activities could create even more customer value. Corporate "mashups" are another good example in the real estate business. By integrating topographic maps from Google in real estate advertisements, Zillow.com gave potential home buyers easy access to market conditions and prices, introducing real added value for customers. Many competitors followed, including DIY selling sites like myproprio.com, where people sell their houses directly without the help of a professional.

Remember, the Best Companies Are Generous

What better way is there to conclude this chapter on value and values than with a quote from David Cameron: "Markets are a means to an end. . . . it's very important we bring a sense of values and a sense of morality to [them]."[28] It is also extremely important to open minds and business territories to enhance efficiency and productivity. The name of the game is to create even more customer value, to make sure it is perceived as such by the final customer, and to deliver products and services at a low cost, which means a fair price. Yes, customer value creation dominates business. Building profitability without cutting customer value is the key challenge.

The best companies are generous. They create a virtuous circle because they believe generosity is a strategic business decision. It is a critical input to business success. They care not only about the quality of what they serve but also about the quality of the way they serve. They have a heart, and their customers and communities know it. They earn a social profit. It is a form of profit sharing, except the profits are not just financial and the beneficiaries are not limited to the organization and the shareholders.[29]

If customer satisfaction and loyalty is so important, why then are so many companies infuriating their customers? Because, unfortunately, it pays. Many firms discovered, for example, just how profitable penalties can be. Some systematically charge extra fees. Banks excel at such unfair practices. But there is a cost. Dissatisfaction and churn (or attrition) should be particularly worrisome to firms whose customers are defecting to competitors offering a transparent, friendly alternative.[30]

CHAPTER 4

Re-Reinventing Business Models

> What is called the music business today, however, is not the business of producing music. At some point, it became the business of selling CDs in plastic cases, and that business will soon be over. But that's not bad news for music, and it's certainly not bad news for musicians.
>
> —Thom Yorke, Radiohead frontman, quoted in *Wired*[1]

Because the world is in a constant state of disruption, it is crucial for business models to be able to integrate new ecosystems.[2] The invention (or reinvention) of business models is a hot topic. This process is highly sensitive and at times emotional because it usually hurts all the employees and forces them to abandon the old values inherent in the previous organizational culture. Many fundamentals of organizations are being scrutinized. Breakthrough thinking from inside or outside the box is critical for one to adapt the business processes of any company not only to the emergence of new technologies but also to the resulting radical behavioral and attitudinal changes among the customers. Companies must define their missions and activities in a new global, but still local, hypercompetitive environment.

Researchers who examine business models usually have very high expectations, and try hard to generate high-quality results. Inversely, the reviewers of publications dealing with this subject are equally critical and demanding, so not many of the researches are meeting their expectations. Although the proposed business models outline useful approaches, most management theory readers often view them as only an incremental advance in conventional wisdom. The literature on business models is rife with paradoxes. The categorization of studies of business models is vague, despite several attempts to establish formal categories and their relationships. Major differences between types of models are not particularly clear in the minds of the potential users. This situation might be explained by the fact that business models are developed to meet different objectives. Some models are extremely useful for analyzing the competitiveness of a company. The concept of value chain associated with Michael Porter's five force analysis (an important framework and tool of analysis for assessing the potential of profitability in an industry) is probably the best example:[3] bargaining power of customers; bargaining power of suppliers; threat of new entrants; threat of substitute products, and competitive rivalry within an industry Should five force analysis really be considered a business model? It seems to be much closer to an analytical business framework and consequently an outstanding tool to establish a diagnosis or prognosis of a company's competitive position. In contrast, other business models (sound and otherwise) try to set out the steps executives should follow to develop a new-to-the-world business model.[4] Some of them introduce systematic ways to assess and refine new business models before someone invests a dime.[5] Business invention is also presented in the "made easy way."[6] Other models are incremental only; they focus on the long-term adaptation, or systematic reinvention, of a new business model starting with an old one. They assume that the best performing corporations are those that constantly review and update their business models to adapt to changing conditions. They ultimately link market share development directly[7] or indirectly to profitability.[8] Paradoxically, the concept of "excellence" in business performance, as the central point of reference, is elusive. The supposedly best performing corporations often sustained a sharp and enduring decline one year later.[9] In another category of business models, the approach is much more disruptive. The focus might be the impact of going global[10] and learning how to do business in a so-called "flat" world. They also highlight the impact of digital technologies and the related deployment of the networked economy. The development of business models then centers on technology, and the main shift is from the real world to a virtual one.[11, 12] Sometimes, the investigation is extended to even more hazardous areas, such as open business models.[13] Other business researchers have looked at the sustainability of business models. Usually, they focus on a specific dimension, such as the sustainability of a high quality of service over time.[14] Still other business models pertain to a specific sector such as services[15, 16] or to a particular concept such as the "loyalty effect."[17] Of course, the lessons learned in the services sector might be extended to more tangible industrial sectors, such as durable products. To summarize, benchmarking one business model to another, without taking into consideration the category to which the model belongs (analytical only, disruptive or incremental innovation, global- or technology-oriented, specialized in a specific area, or linked to a unique business concept, etc.), is inadequate. Comparing business models is definitely challenging.

Surprisingly, one important point has never been raised. If the titles of the publications on business models are any indication, the ultimate objective is profit making. Competitive advantage, business model design, business performance, and all the other criteria of success in business are apparently driven only (or mainly) by profits. I strongly believe that profits should not be the primary objective in business. Rather, profitability should be viewed as the reward for customer satisfaction, not the other way around! Of course, a business model needs to be profitable. All the same, of the books that assert that creating customer value is the first priority to succeed in business, very few convey this message in their titles.[18] If you have any doubt about this, simply do a search for business models online and see for yourself.

It's no wonder many reviewers repeat that nothing is really new. Again and again, business researchers are highlighting, in all honesty, the primacy of customer value creation, but they often reduce it to one of the key results of their analysis. They do not insist that CVC is the top objective. Could customer value creation be that hard to sell? Promoting profit making is much easier, as I can attest from my professional experience. This mismatch between the reality of business management and the covers of business books encourages shortsightedness. That is a pity.

In this chapter, I am not trying to "reinvent the reinvention" of business models. Nor am I reinventing the wheel. My vision stands out because I affirm that customer value creation should be companies' ultimate goal. CVC should thus be the cornerstone of all business models, affecting daily management, model development, and their blueprint or formulations on paper. I go beyond simply linking a specific business process development method to CVC, as "Six Sigma" links profitable growth to CVC.[19]

Many participants in my marketing seminars have complained that explaining the positive link between CVC and financial performance is daunting because there are too many finance people in the audience. Yes, it is quite difficult to discuss the CVC-oriented approach in front of executives, especially if they are under highly competitive pressure and are afraid of losing their jobs. But, once again, the underlying philosophy of this book is that CVC is the top priority. Because of the commoditization of markets and because financial performance is considered a reward, the gap between top and worst performers in customer satisfaction is increasing steadily, fueled by hypercompetition and customer empowerment. The unique ten-year study of the evolution of the American Customer Satisfaction Index by the University of Michigan is revealing; their results are unequivocal.[20] The results clearly demonstrate the close relationship between the financial performance of a company and the level of customer satisfaction. The data are valid internally and externally and the facts are well presented: they clearly demonstrate the close relationship between the financial performance of a company and the level of customer satisfaction. The positive relationship between the two variables is increasing because people have the choice. If they are not satisfied with a company they can switch easily: they have the choice.

To succeed in business, executives must believe in customer satisfaction. They simply have no alternative. We will revisit this argument in the conclusion. In essence, in corporate leadership, it is vital that the fundamental attitude toward the clients be positive.

To follow the previous chapter logically and unwaveringly, I present a specific category of business models below. I explain the steps to follow in the reinvention of a business model under pressure from commoditization. Customer value creation (CVC) is the ultimate objective. It will be incorporated in the definition of a solid customer value proposition (CVP). All the functions of a company, including

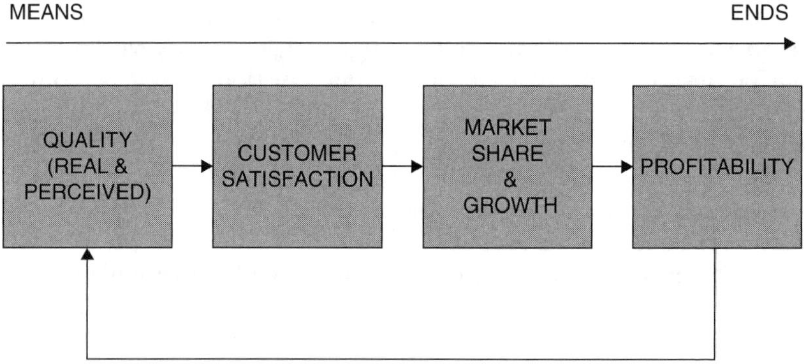

Figure 4.1 The basic vision of the value chain.

finance, will be integrated in the definition, as will their specific contributions to value creation. The result will be a collage of all the business functions in search of synergies. Adequate cost designing, rather than systematic cost cutting, will allow truly efficient and responsible executives to build honest, well-deserved profitability (see figure 4.1).

The Epic Battle Between Innovation and the Status Quo

Resistance to change has always existed. It has been called the battle between the forces of conservatism and the forces of modernism. This phenomenon is also observable in market segmentation. Some people are open to change; others are not. Some cities are cosmopolitan and their residents crave novelties and the latest fashions, whereas in other cities, residents behave like followers. Even countries can be clustered according to their openness to change or their innovation proneness. Greece is a country with very high risk avoidance. Innovation is not their cup of tea, and resistance to change is noticeable. Conversely, highly risk tolerant countries are eager to change radically and fast. South Korea, despite its strong cultural traditions, is turned to the future. They invent the future (as Samsung's motto says). Or they certainly try!

Resistance to change is more than a cultural trait. It might be a limitation in the human mind. Just because you are a true innovator does not mean you will be a visionary. Many inventors do not foresee the future developments of their own inventions. Just think of some of the famous, now laughable, predictions. In 1943, Thomas Watson, then chairman of IBM, forecast a world market of about five computers. In 1981, Microsoft founder Bill Gates said 640K would be enough memory for anyone.

Because the development of novelties is disruptive, it might be perceived as a threat. A good example is the negative reactions of a French telecom company to the development of the Internet in the country. They were marketing a basic version of a connection system called the "Minitel." It consisted of a terminal with a black-and-white screen operating on a phone line, which allowed people to connect to some sites with very limited interactivity. The system was initially very profitable for the company, acting as a cash cow in their portfolio. They naturally did everything they could to delay the implementation of cables designed to support high-speed Internet. The company executives knew that the speed and volume capacity of the connection is directly related to the intensity of Internet usage, especially for e-commerce. Their business model was attacked from all sides, and they had no viable short-term counterresponse. They sustained the Minitel for as long as they could. Despite the current downturn, e-commerce in France has truly taken off. The high-speed cable network is finally in place.

An excellent book about the evolution of an entire industry and its consequences on business models is *Inventing the Movies* by Scott Kirsner.[21] The book describes the development of new business models in the movie industry, studded with epic battles between innovation and the status quo. It paints a compelling picture that can be easily extrapolated to other economic sectors. It also reveals the impact of technological changes on well-entrenched business models.

The real enemy of progress may not be the fear of technological change per se but rather the fear of undermining a successful business model. Often, executives are more concerned with the flow of money between various internal and external components (and economic actors) of a business model. The more the overall system is buttressed, hermetically sealed, and highly profitable for all the "partners," the greater the resistance to change. Resistance is a way to protect the goose that lays the golden eggs.[22] It results in conflicting and sometimes highly subjective visions of the future. The Internet could be a boon for Hollywood if the industry can overcome its fears.[23]

As turbulence rages, ludicrous "anti-leak" overreactions often surface. Take the music industry. The Mytunes revolution (a software release in 2003 that allows Windows users to download digital music) has ramped up the pressure. The strategies of the major labels (companies and renowned artists) to preserve the status quo in the industry are ineffectual. They need to find new ways to adapt. Thousands of songs in your pocket might seem like nothing new, but it has taken more than four decades of breakthroughs in audio technologies to get there. We will never listen to music the same way again.[24]

The publishing industry is also being affected. Will books go digital? There is resistance to this trend because many consumers still enjoy the feeling of owning and reading a traditional book. The question is how long will the current model remain unchanged? Freedom of the press is also being challenged. Traditional media—from newspapers to radio stations and television channels—are being forced to rethink their business models. Media companies can no longer bury their heads in the sand. It is too late for them to simply wait and see. Things are changing too fast. The giants of the stock photo business are also contending with a horde of "micro-stock" agencies, which are forcing them to revise their business models. Selling photographs is becoming a game almost anyone can play.[25] In fact, the real concern is how technology is revolutionizing the business of information.[26]

Even highly protected areas like telemedicine are shifting radically. The future of medicine may lie closer to home.[27] This new high-tech approach permits remote consultations by video link. Remote surgery is feasible! Satellite-Internet connections are changing the way doctors work. Medical institutions will have to be managed by experts in IT deployment. Even if such technologies make doctors' work and patients' lives easier while increasing accessibility to medicine for the masses and possibly reducing costs, some doctors and specialists are still fighting such developments aggressively. They are mainly afraid of losing control. They do not want telemedicine to become a household product. They will not be able to stop the revolution, although they might delay it unnecessarily.

Bank and credit card companies are extremely concerned, too. It is not only about the potential side effects of regulation. What will be the future of money? Cash, checks, and credit cards—who will need them in the near future? Currency is flexible and frictionless, and it might become (almost) free.[28] What if people could transfer money over Twitter for next to nothing? The idea of moving money that quickly and cheaply is not ridiculous anymore.

The Elements of a Successful Business Model: CVP at the Core

It all starts with strategic innovation

To fight the effects of commoditization and the downturn, strategic innovation in business is crucial. Though many studies have provided insight into specific aspects of innovation, they offer only partial solutions to the overall problems managers are facing. A much more general perspective on innovation is needed. It should include a wide range of innovation in techniques, products, processes, administration, and so on. That is why innovation should be conceived as a multidimensional concept. All the dimensions must be reintegrated in a meaningful model, centralized around a strategic priority acting as a cornerstone and fostering internal synergies between the dimensions and efficient external relationships with the ecosystem.

Strategic innovation is the source of four main benefits for businesses.[29] First, it allows the opening or redefinition of new market spaces, boundaries, or territories. Second, it sidelines competition. It is always much more difficult to copy and match a successful overall strategic innovation than a specific one with limited scope. Third, it frequently creates higher value for the customer at a lower cost. As mentioned, strategic innovation is the best response to the new economic reality. Lastly, it might foster profitable growth. Building profitability during the reinvention of any business model is crucial. When combined, cost designing (instead of cost cutting) and building profitability (instead of profit making) are the two best ways to deliver what the customer expects at a low cost.

The underlying philosophy behind innovation as a main driver of business growth states that dogma must be rooted out and a new future imagined and invented.[30, 31] It is about who "gets to the future first," management consultants Gary Hamel and C. K. Prahalad argued.[32] In "Competing for the Future," they urged companies to create their own futures, envision new markets, and reinvent themselves. Granted, this is extremely difficult. Basically, the idea is to develop and evaluate business strategy for "new game" situations that are not well aligned with traditional business strategy. A fundamental reconceptualization of a business strategy must translate into the design of a blueprint for a new or reinvented business model.

Followed by the Business Model (Definition and Components)

Configuring a business model means operationalizing strategic innovation. You must build a bridge between the strategy and each function of an organization. The model translates strategic innovation into architecture with financial, structural, and commercial dimensions. This value-oriented architecture combines different types of value, notably customer value, chain value, and financial value.

Online queries about business models turn up two million hits, but surprisingly few articles have focused on this concept. Consequently, although the term "business model" is often used these days, it is seldom defined explicitly. The most-cited definition is that of Timmers: "A business model includes the architecture for the product or service, an information flow, a description of the benefits for the business actors involved, and a description of the sources of revenue."[33]

Business models have three basic components:[34]

1) the value proposition, comprising the targeted type of customer or the market segment addressed by the business activity, the product or service, and partners who create a link between the business and the customer;
2) the value architecture, comprising the company's resources, internal value chain, and external value chain (i.e., all the links with partners, suppliers, etc.)
3) the revenue model: the cost structure, the monetary value captured by the business, and the profit.

In recent years, the concept of the business model has largely centered on value creation and appropriation. Thus, a business model is the representation of a firm's underlying logic and strategic choices to create and capture value within an existing or emerging ecosystem by manipulating the three basic components just mentioned.[35] Because value appropriation has been the key driver of business models, compounded by the increasing pressure of commoditization, particularly the quest to reduce margins, the vision of business models has been narrowed to focus on cash acquisition. The business model concept thus spells out how a company makes money by situating itself in the value chain. Rather than trying to help the company gain a traditional competitive advantage, it stresses the revenue generation process and its consequences on profit appropriation.[36] The business model concept can be reduced to a simple question: How can I make money in my industry? The third basic component of our previous list—profit—thus becomes the sole priority.

It has taken researchers many years to give value creation its rightful place in the reinvention of a business model.

The Reinvention of Customer-Oriented Business Models

A recent study by the American Management Association found that multinationals channel only 10 percent of total investment into developing new business models. Yet everyone is talking about this reinvention. The same paradox applies to the prevalence of a customer-centric orientation. Too many publications have neglected the customer aspect: they talk about what the model does for the business, not for the customer. Yet this too is a very popular topic.[37] The same pattern is seen in the execution of cost-cutting initiatives versus the attempt to achieve profitable growth. On a scale of 1 to 10, with 10 being excellent, it is estimated that, on average, companies rank near 8 on cost cutting and closer to 2 on achieving profitable growth.

Such disparities cannot persist. Commoditization combined with megatrends like the increasing pace and magnitude of economic crises and the radical evolution in the configuration of competitive markets around the world demand more sound business approaches. They are slowly emerging. Obviously, it is difficult for economic, business, and finance actors to give up their old (bad) habits.

As part of the harmonious development of a new global economy, one that is more responsible for its actions, the focus must be on profitable growth rather than on generation of short-term profits. This is because short-term profits can only be achieved at the expense of other peoples or other markets. These markets were often located abroad, and globalization was supposed to benefit only the U.S. large multinationals and their home country. The problem is the unexpected consequences. Discontent is escalating, and people are becoming increasingly outspoken.

Large investments in cost cutting only, even effective ones, have not generated gains in strategic advantages or driven profitable growth. Yet many companies are understandably reluctant to leave their comfort zone and try to understand their customers better.[38]

When they try to tackle these problems, senior executives at incumbent companies find that internal and external stakeholders consider new business models unattractive. To enter the land of the "new," they need a roadmap, which consists of four simple steps defined in an outstanding article published in December 2008 by Johnson, Christensen, and Kagermann.[39]

The starting idea is that breakthrough, game-changing products rarely emerge from established businesses. That is because a radically new product usually needs a new business model. In fact, success starts by not thinking about business models at all, but rather by thinking about the opportunity to satisfy a real customer who needs a job done.

Here are the steps to reinvent a business model:

1) Start by developing a strong customer value proposition (CVP). What can you provide customers in order to help them find a real, trustable solution to their problems in a given situation?

The authors refer to a "job done" by the customer. It is obvious that the offering will be designed according to the kind of help the customers expect. The higher the expectations, the lower the level of customer satisfaction with the current options and the greater the impact the CVP will have on the customer. The definition of a CVP is much more than the establishment of a unique selling proposition (USP) or the formulation of a positioning statement. It integrates, from the start, all the functions and tools the companies will use to solve the problem of the targeted customers, with the purpose of helping them solve a problem and get their "job" done.

2) Construct a profit formula that allows you to deliver value to your company. The goal is to design a blueprint that defines how the company creates value for itself while providing the customer with value. Making a profit is only one piece of the model. The authors of the article speak of "building profitability." This approach is most useful when setting the price of the CVP. During this phase, the components consist of the revenue model, the cost structure, the margin model, and the resource velocity.
3) Look for key resources, that is to say, for assets such as people, technologies, facility equipment, channels, and brands required to deliver the customer value proposition to the targeted segment.
4) Envision key operational processes because, in every business model, execution is fundamental. Focus on both implementation and execution. Successful companies have unique processes that are hard for the competitors to reproduce. Such processes might apply to sectors such as logistics, manufacturing, budgeting, and training.

At first glance, this framework might appear simple (see figure 4.2), but it is not. The underlying strength lies in the complex interdependence of its parts. I call it the final collage. This process is exemplified in the case of Zara, presented later in this chapter. Dell and Gateway are other examples of competitors using the same business model with varying degrees of success. Both companies were applying the direct sales model in the computer sector. For many years, Dell has been profitable while Gateway floundered and was absorbed by Acer. The cost structure was not as good at Gateway as it was at Dell, and that destroyed the bottom line. Costs were a major difference between the two companies.

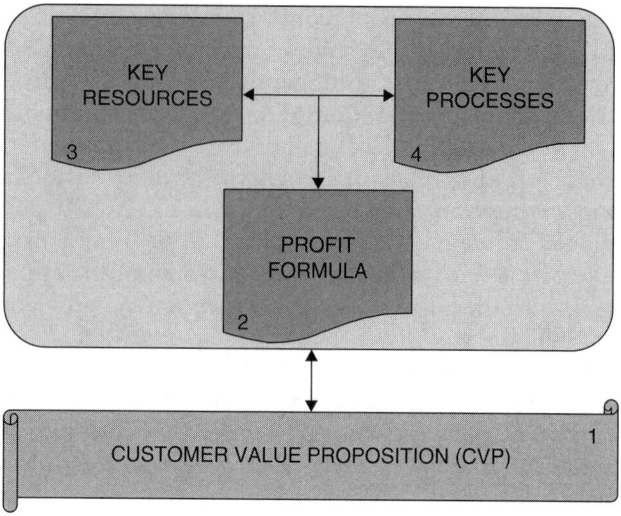

Figure 4.2 Reinventing your business model and making it customer-centric.

Finally, it is advisable that you weigh your reinvented model against your current one. It is critical to know if you can implement the revised model within your organization or if you should set up a separate unit. This thorny issue will be discussed below.

This fundamental model of business reinvention embodies the underlying business philosophy of this book: making customer value creation the main driver of profitable growth. Creating value is not about devising a new series of management tools. As some authors rightly point out, believing in CVC and acting accordingly requires a profound leap in business mentalities.[40] The leap is to put the customer value proposition first and only then to design a profitable engine in which value will be shared between all the parties in the business model and the company's ecosystem. This is the only way to achieve truly profitable growth.

The Link Between CVC and CVP

Customer value creation is a disciplined approach to profitable growth that has been used successfully by many companies. There is still room for significant improvement, as relatively few companies endorse this approach and act accordingly. Economic downturns tend to freeze positive development by causing executives to revert to an inside-out approach, namely to what has served companies well during the previous crisis: significantly reducing their costs. Now cost cutting has reached its limit, and it is time for an outside-in perspective to take precedence. The objective is to improve the company's position in a perspective of customer-driven demand.

To apply a CVC approach thoroughly, one needs to do an extensive customer value analysis (CVA). The term "value" in CVA is defined by the customer, not by executives. Value has to be perceived as such by the customer. This is why extensive analysis of customer behaviors and attitudes is an absolute prerequisite. The next chapter focuses on customer-centered innovation, particularly the ways executives can determine what the customers consider valuable by understanding their daily experiences and identifying breakthrough potential for new products or services.

Before investigating CVC and innovation further, I define the overall equation between customer value creation, the customer value proposition (CVP), and the overall business execution. My formula is inspired by the CVC formula introduced by Plaster and Alderman.[41] The two main differences are that the originators of the formula did not refer to CVP. Their brilliant concepts are specifically linked to the "Six Sigma" approach. I use CVP in connection with the model of Johnson, Christensen, and Kagermann, and my approach is more general (see figure 4.3).

Figures 4.2 and 4.3 explain the phenomenal success of the women's apparel retailer Zara.

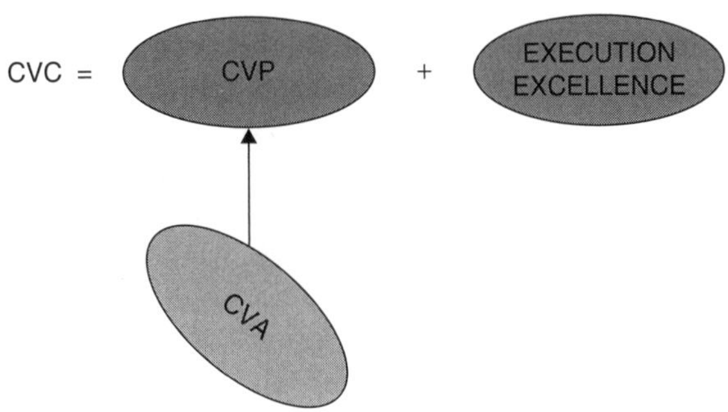

Figure 4.3 The customer value creation formula (and process).

The Final Collage: Value and Glue ("The Zara Way")

Zara, owned by Inditex, stands out because of several astute, reinforcing business model building blocks. The company was conceived and built along a vertically integrated demand and supply chain, whereas most other textile chains rely on outsourcing and cheap labor in China. Zara studies its customers' demand in the stores and tries to instantly adapt to the latest trends and deliver as fast as possible. This gives them a particularly appealing value proposition: an easy-access collection that is in line with the very latest fashion. The *Economist* writes, "When Madonna gave a series of concerts in Spain, teenage girls were able to spot at her last performance the outfit she wore for her first concert, thanks to Zara."[42] It takes the company only five weeks to come up with a new garment from design to delivery and only two weeks to receive an existing model.

There is another customer value proposition that makes Zara irresistible to shoppers. The company changes its clothing assortments on a weekly basis and sometimes on a store-by-store basis. This product policy increases the perceived risk of missing what you had always been looking for. Marketing experts working in retail have quipped that women are more loyal to the delivery truck than to the banner! Some customers know the schedule of deliveries to their favorite store, and they visit it accordingly to preserve their first mover priority. It is the best guarantee of a full choice. If you missed something, you will never find it again.

Zara's business model has been analyzed extensively. The studies unanimously conclude that the operational execution at Zara delivers what customers are expecting at an attractive cost, allowing the company to build profitability.

Their headquarters are located in the Spanish countryside, where the price per square foot is low, much cheaper than downtown Madrid or even Barcelona. Their designers and salespeople collaborate. They work in the same area of the building. Many companies use the reverse approach: people in R&D do not mix with sales agents or with marketing people. Marketing people do not even interact much with salespeople!

Zara stores, in contrast, are located at prestigious addresses known for high fashion: Rue de Rivoli in Paris and Fifth Avenue in New York. In the stores, the merchandising is driven by a selective approach. Their retail strategy gives customers the feeling they are in a deluxe area but at an affordable price. In 2008, they ran 11 factories to increase the production speed for small series. They react fast. The in-store design is centralized in Arteixo (a city in north-west Spain) to decrease costs and maintain the homogeneity of the brand codes.[43]

It is obvious that Zara has not succeeded simply by chance. The entire business has been revised. They do not follow the traditional pattern of the industry: one collection for spring and summer, another collection for fall and winter. Some people say they are simply copycats. They can also be considered very open to inspiration. The time between designing a sketch for a model and hanging the item in a store is at most several weeks. They flout the rules, invent the future, and are building a new configuration for an entire seemingly frozen industry. Despite this audacity, even Zara has a rival fast approaching: H&M.

Organization Integration: Watch Your Step!

The CEO of a large industrial printing company recently told me that he felt relieved because he decided to preserve his offset division despite the success of his new digital printing business unit. He admitted his traditional offset activities were not very profitable, but they generated a lot of volume and added to his fixed costs. The more valuable and profitable digital activities were attractive. They allow the company to present customized solutions to the customers, create considerable customer value, and generate profitable growth. All the same, they had not yet reached the overall volume of the offset. The recently acquired digital technology was already obsolete, and sizeable investments were needed.

The insertion of a new business model in an existing organization always causes huge ripples. It might be stressful, too, because it raises fundamental questions about the future of the entire organization. These concerns are not limited to the new business model. Internal adjustments may also cause an upheaval. Many companies assume that once they have introduced a major innovation, growth will follow. It's not that simple. High-potential new businesses within established companies face stiff headwinds well after their inception.[44]

Specialty chemicals giant Dow Corning caught its competitors by surprise in 2002 when it launched Xiameter, a discount Web-based sales channel with a no-frills selling and delivery approach. Their mandate was to bring in new business and retain cost-conscious customers who were fleeing their traditional, high-touch relationship with the company, wherein there is an effort to cultivate a close relationship with customers asking for assistance. The new strategy for marketing commodity silicones has been too successful. It was supposed to de-bundle peripheral services and to offer a no-frills service at a very competitive price. The problem is that even in the B2B area, buyers made the connection between Dow Corning and Xiameter. The no-frills customer value proposition became very attractive to traditional buyers, too, at the expense of the existing bundling activities. Internal cross-cannibalization then appeared between the traditional and the new business models. Even worse, the no-frills buyers suddenly started to ask for better service at nearly the same price, which they were not supposed to do. The reason is simple: the competition reacted to Xiameter by launching their own Web sites. They matched their prices, but they also offered extra services. Now Dow Corning is facing a delicate situation. The question is this: Should they allow Xiameter to offer peripheral services, which were supposed to be exclusive to their traditional activities?[45, 46]

Changing the rules of business is not a self-contained decision. It is very hard to control the side effects in general and the potential diffusion to other business units. Customer empowerment invariably takes a heavy toll on a company. Hypercompetition undermines the sustainability of a competitive advantage. Sooner than expected, a copycat might emerge with an even better offer. Your specialty will revert to a commodity sooner than expected, and you will have to rethink your business model. Welcome to the wacky world of business model reinvention!

Long-Term Viability: Sustaining Does Not Mean Freezing

The longevity of success is not guaranteed. The definition of commoditization and the description of its origins, presented in chapter 2, emphasize that a key dimension is the breakneck pace of innovation.

Because innovation is at the very center of all business activities, strategic development or reinvention of business models is essential. Executives should keep in mind that, like products, models begin as specialties but may quickly become commonplace, like commodities.

The concept of reinventing business models is intellectually very attractive. It is also extremely complex. This is why building a successful model is so rewarding. Yet success might be ephemeral. In managing their product or service portfolio, executives must learn how to sell commodities profitably and how to benefit from specialties as long as possible. Business models follow a similar evolution. Overprotecting a business model might be a severe mistake. Freezing and desperately patching holes are not the solution.

Difficulties aside, there is one point every executive should keep in mind. It is always harder to copy a successful business model than it is a product, service, or process. With time, copying is feasible and inevitable. Commoditization is not limited to products or services. It is a pandemic that afflicts business models as well.

PART 3

Reversing the Tide of Commoditization Constructively

CHAPTER 5

An Integrated Set of New Business Logics

Does this crisis give socialism a better name? No. It gives regulated capitalism a better name.

—Paul Krugman[1]

Earlier in this book, commoditization was defined, explained, and clarified. Its major impacts on the economy and on business practices have been clarified. The diagnosis and prognosis of its consequences on growth and profitability have also been laid out extensively. The prerequisites for decision making on value creation have been honestly and transparently justified. Consistent with the intellectual process of this book, we will now move from ideas to action and present strategic recommendations on customer value creation, specifically how to develop it, how to translate it into a strong CVP, how to keep it relevant, and how to avoid leakage of value by determining where cuts will hurt customer perceptions.

Reversing the tide of commoditization is admittedly not easy. Creating and delivering customer value is a challenge. As a business goal, meeting customer expectations at a low cost is even harder nowadays than it was several years ago. To improve their chances of success, it is extremely important for companies and executives to avoid four major pitfalls.

The first mistake is trying to fight commoditization by deploying business actions limited to one aspect of a company or to one function. As I explained, managing commoditization and value creation is definitely not restricted to cost management; neither is it exclusive to marketing, or to logistics, and so on. All silo-type (i.e., narrow-minded) reasoning will inevitably lead to failure. The best approach is to consider the entire organization—in other words, use the business model framework of analysis. As chapter 4 underlines, only highly innovative business models drive both growth and share value on the stock market, much more effectively than business models whose focus of innovation is restricted to a specific area of uniqueness, such as original products, pleasant customer experience, or lean business processes. The notion of an integrated collage built around CVP is crucial. To avoid the pitfall of a limited business model, the restricted approach of value-based marketing is repositioned within a larger one, where it is transformed into a more inclusive value-driven business approach.

The second pitfall appears when people try to change their business approach without modifying their traditional corporate goals and attitudes. They are simply putting new wine in old bottles. They are not adapting their ideas or paradigms. They tweak some of their peripheral perspectives to avoid dissonance with their core business habits. It is less disruptive for them, but most often it is not effective. Too many executives still expect that their customers will realign, and usually they don't. They do very little soul searching or none at all. They are locked in a reactive mode. To illustrate this pitfall from a marketing perspective, we will reexamine the real meaning of engaging, or reengaging, the customer.

The third pitfall is another crucial one. It involves understanding precisely where cuts will hurt customers' perceptions of value and adversely affect their buying behavior. If this distinction is not made wisely, important investments will not have a lasting effect, while low-value projects will endure.[2] Such mistakes notably occur in marketing and sales. You can cut marketing or sales costs as long as you are not stunting revenues.

The fourth and final pitfall is the fact that the quest for a strong and appealing CVP is, for many companies, little more than hopeful sifting through customer interviews. It is more important than ever to discover opportunities for breakthrough products and services by trying to pinpoint the job a customer is trying to get done and offering efficient solutions. More systematic inquiries are necessary to uncover the best ideas that should be considered as an exhaustive set of growth opportunities.[3]

The end of this chapter features general roadmaps for action in an integrated set of logics developed during the past ten years. The integration of these logics is a way to establish a comprehensive action-oriented framework in order to reinvent business models, be creative, and support the value-for-money perspective. The next chapter, preceding the conclusion, systematically examines ways (some more disruptive than others) to create customer value and to formulate a strong customer value proposition, and it provides the practical recommendations executives seek.

The CVP-Driven Business Model

The concept of value-based marketing is not new. Fortunately, it is increasingly capturing the attention of companies across various industries. The increased interest in value-based marketing is being stoked by the fierce, global debate among different conceptions of what "value" really stands for. This urgent debate, with its overt sociopolitical tinge, was discussed in chapter 3. Here I define (or reinvent) what value-based marketing really is. Because there are so many different and opposite perspectives on this issue, the obvious question is this: Is there a dominant perspective?

I will answer this basic and quite fundamental question methodically by going through a step-by-step approach. The outcome will be a revised definition of value-based marketing backed by sound argumentation.

The first step is to determine if it is possible to speak of value-based marketing with the underlying idea that the marketing function should play a pivotal role in the creation of shareholder value as the top priority.[4] It is definitively not possible because this exclusive position contradicts the inherent priorities that define marketing as a business process: creating customer satisfaction first by providing real and perceived value. Remember, achieving growth and profits is the reward, not the reverse (as explained earlier).

The second step is to envision values-based marketing, instead of value-based marketing. Doing so depends on whether core values are closely linked to business management and corporate orientations. Customer satisfaction is a priority at the product or service level (performance and quality levels must meet the expectations of the targeted segment). Defining values in business is by definition a much more long-term issue than creating customer satisfaction, which is about day-to-day operations (and consequently hard to sustain in the medium and long terms). Common examples include Ben & Jerry's Ice Cream and The Body Shop. Consumers buy from them based as much on an emotional connection with protecting the earth and animal rights as on their satisfaction with the ice cream and the cosmetics.[5]

The third step is to define what value stands for from a strict customer perspective. A two-sided or shared perspective is needed. In a relationship between a company and its customers, mutual respect and trust should prevail, as should shared responsibility for reaching a fair balance between customer expectations and supplier performance. A company should not educate customers, especially if the customers don't ask it to. An overall commitment to impact the customer positively and constructively should prevail, which is the opposite of manipulation or marketing tricks. We all know how such harmful practices negatively affect the marketing function. Companies must adopt a fundamental business attitude that contains the following steps: commit to the most important things that will impact your customers, create customer value that is meaningful and understandable, and assess how you did at creating true customer value. Only then will the bottom line be profitable.[6]

The concept of value-based marketing is difficult to grasp because it is inherently misleading. There are contradictions between the in-depth meanings of the concepts and the time perspectives—short or long term. Value-based marketing should be replaced by value-based business management with a (dominant) marketing perspective. The reinvention of business models should be driven by a strong willingness and commitment in the corporate culture (and related mission statement) to provide value, as perceived by the customer, including values, with an appropriate and honest marketing plan to deliver it (strategies and tactics). The customer value proposition, which is the very first step in the reinvention of business models, not only identifies the job to be done for the targeted consumers but also proposes a solution in keeping with values such as ecology, fair trade, and social causes.

Value-based marketing, as a specialized business process, must be repositioned. It should be replaced by CVP-driven business management. Reframing and revising the approach increases the logic because the final formula translates the internal and connected realities of the company coherently. The CVP should be the centerpiece of the reinvention of a business model. Marketing is included in the overall corporate strategy of the company. The distinction between long-term orientations in term of values and short-term delivery of value in day-to-day marketing management is thus taken into account. Lastly, the major vision of a business model is holistic rather than focusing on a particular business function, including marketing. If it is true that marketing should be considered as strategy[7] and not be restricted to the four Ps, neither should it be envisioned as the predominant function.

This perception leads to arrogant attitudes by marketers and to the misconception of the marketing department as an ivory tower. Arrogant marketers do not listen to their customers because they think they don't have to. They believe they know what is good or bad for their customers, and of course, they are totally wrong!

"Engage Marketing": A Mirage?

Engaging the customer has been touted by some experts as the way to reinvent marketing for today's connected, collaborative, and hyperinteractive culture.[8] The idea is very attractive, but its implementation might be limited. In the following paragraphs, I discuss and clarify the importance of engaging consumers.

As underlined in the previous chapters, customers are more empowered than ever, and the Web is a vast place where people can meet and chat. But the idea of the Web as a forum where people create and learn is not borne out in reality. The creative and educational use of the Web seems to be limited to a minority of users, to specific interest groups or to specific situations in which the arousal or the need to participate is highest. Buying a new car generates a lot of online information search activities, both passive and active. Providing adequate information through multiple Web sites is a great source of value creation for a car manufacturer. A health problem will create an understandable eagerness to learn about symptoms, possible remedies, and so on. Discussing potential treatments is another valuable way to respond to the needs of involved customers, as patients, and to provide them with sound recommendations. Crowd-sourcing has interesting potential to tap collective intelligence online,[9] but it is certainly not as widespread as some claim. No one is questioning the wisdom of the masses or trying to prolong the debate between a socialist and a capitalistic vision.[10] Just because the concept of crowd-sourcing is at odds with centuries of practice, it need not be dismissed because of preconceived notions.[11] All the same, it is hard to understand if and how this new generation of potential customers collaborates, shares, and creates.[12]

Do people want to be systematically "engaged" with companies as potential customers? Clearly, consumers have evolved from passive viewers and choosers into active and powerful audiences. Some of them participate and collaborate in crowd-sourcing activities (R&D, advertising copy development). Engaging such audiences might give you the keys to success. Yet permission is fundamental to marketing.[13]

The problem is that customers do not grant permission that easily. This creates a real gap between theory and practice. You can't "engage" your customers by force. Godin's latest advice about change is shocking.[14] He said that change isn't brought about by asking permission. Change happens when you ask for forgiveness. That may be true, but his advice should be followed with extreme caution. When one is dealing with online communities, it is a good way to create major problems.

In some ways, the concept of "engage marketing" seems like trying to reinvent an old way of doing things when the audience clamors for a radically different approach. It is precisely because we are facing a totally new environment, moving from uniform mass markets (like the hit era of the 1950s that was characterized by a limited number of hit songs wherein the same type of music was being played out from the same radio stations; this was quite a uniform and mass marketing scene) into a mass market of one (the underground era wherein people can now access rare songs by connecting to multiple Web sites), that businesspeople have to change not only their approaches to customer value creation (the tools) but also their initial goals (short-term profit making). Many large companies have gradually lost control. Engaging customers does not mean "reengaging" them. It is time to adopt a new perspective and attitude toward the marketing practice.

Let's take an example. Marketers must adapt by joining the rich, deep, and meaningful conversation already in progress over the Internet.[15] Marketers must do everything they can to become a welcome and invited part of the dialogue. But they have to understand that the resulting partnership must provide win-win situations and shared results. It is not just about endlessly selling more and more stuff to people! Too many companies only want to regain control. They have not learned anything from their mistakes. Not surprisingly, this is an extremely sensitive and emotional subject in the business world. For too long, economic development has been based only on boosting consumption, without any limits. Excessive pressure to consume explains why economists and executives are finding it so hard to shrug off deeply anchored attitudes and behaviors, even though they must. This problem is much more pronounced in North America than in Europe. North American economists and businesspeople must understand that the customer empowerment is irreversible. Customers are reacting against any attempts to control them or infiltrate their communities of friends because many of them are "engaged in disengagement"! Remember the "bacon affair," a spontaneous and strong rebellion by Facebook members against an attempt by some companies (including Sony) to infiltrate their communities of friends with the initial blessing of the social Web site. And, by the way, announcing the return of the so-called "hard selling approach" is a rather worrisome matter.[16] Moreover, one wonders why large enterprises (such as Wal-Mart, PepsiCo, and GE) began to recruit the military's elite.[17] This is perhaps done so with the hope that a military approach would make up for the lack of business leadership as far as their control over consumers was concerned, without realizing that customer empowerment is now a reality. Are we selling solutions or will we get back to the approach of selling pressure? One again, the old ghosts come out of the cupboards.

Marketing has moved from a traditional mass marketing approach in which the brand was the equity to a marketing of one, in which case the business model equity is under scrutiny. During this long period (until the 1980s), communication flowed downward, from companies to the customers. Companies were in total control. With the development of relationship marketing, the customer became the equity. Marketing communication changed into a two-way channel. Customers could address the companies directly. Now, in a real digital world, companies are focusing on their business model equity. They are not sure of their overall configuration in the near future. They are facing a new market environment, a mass market of one. Internet users, some of whom reject companies, are exchanging files, products, even services beyond companies' control. There are many examples of people exasperated by financial institutions who are trying to build their own financial communities. They collectively launched Web sites and use them as platforms to extend loans P2P.

These perspectives on equity are complementary not exclusive. Traditional mass marketing will not be "killed" by CRM, as some gurus warn, or be replaced by digital marketing. As a common denominator, customer empowerment is a reality and its force must be recognized. It is certainly not the end of the world. Fighting against it or trying to quell it is useless. The best solution is to adopt a more realistic approach. If you can't beat 'em, join 'em. When consumers you have never met are deriding your company's products in public forums, your company is vulnerable. You need to turn this threat into an opportunity. Learning, instead of trying to fight a virtual opponent, is a much more positive and constructive attitude toward marketing management.[18] For example, using news releases, blogs, podcasting, viral marketing, and online media to reach buyers directly is a sound approach as long as companies produce messages their customers want to hear.[19] The new rules of marketing and PR should be designed to increase customer satisfaction first. Remember, as a representative of a company, you are what you publish on the Internet. People will quickly discover your real intentions. Too many companies are scrambling to discover new leads with the help of online relationships, hoping for profitable-only insights—what a friend is worth in monetary terms.[20] Other companies may try hard to manage tweets, to silence errant messages while exploiting social networks.[21] By acting in this way, they do not have the client at heart. Instead, companies should harness online networks to better serve their customers and to increase their satisfaction, which is the only way to drive their organic growth. Successful innovators can develop products that resonate by connecting deeply with consumers. Staying "tuned in" is a way to keep an organization on its toes and renew a focus on creating the kind of value customers are ready to pay for.[22] Intel's Andy D. Bryant says Web 2.0 is the "Wild, wild west" of corporate life (2009). I agree.

Cutting Sales and Marketing Costs (Not Revenues)

When extraordinary economic forces such as commoditization put pressure on margins, courageous companies can use difficult circumstances to make their operations not only less expensive but also more effective. Less courageous companies will panic and cut costs frenetically and indiscriminately. They are shooting themselves in the foot.

Regrettably, when the decline in revenues and margins is continuous, fear and the belief that it is impossible to provide better value at a low cost (and to be both fast and precise) often results in two sweeping practices: trimming only back-office staff and functions or instituting across-the-board cost cuts, which includes advertising and marketing budgets and front-line sales reps. Such mistakes are understandable, but the results are most often disappointing.

Companies that closely manage their operations related to maintaining their customer value are taking rigorous approaches to resetting their budgets for service, communication, marketing, and sales. They manage to save money without undermining the functions or customer satisfaction. In short, they have carefully measured the "breakpoints" to pinpoint their customers' true sensitivity to change in levels of service.

A wireless telecommunications services provider found that its customers had two breakpoints at X and Y seconds on a call; answering the phone immediately (less than X seconds) produced delight, whereas leaving customers on hold for longer (more than Y seconds) produced strong dissatisfaction. Although customers were fairly indifferent to service levels between X and Y, the company's average time to answer was only loosely managed between the two points. The company considered raising service levels to the "delight breakpoint" or reducing them to just above the "patience threshold." Customer-lifetime-value economics pointed to the second option.[23]

To manage customer value creation effectively, it is important to see marketing and sales budgets as investments, not as expenses. For every investment, it is critical to measure their effectiveness, but this is notoriously difficult.[24] The problem is that many companies are not using the tools available to them. However, some companies that understand their spending well are planning to increase their marketing and sales budgets despite the current economic downturn. By optimizing their budgets instead of cutting them indiscriminately, they create competitive differentiation.[25]

A McKinsey global survey is showing that executives at business-to-consumer (B2C) companies are nearly twice as—likely at 22 percent—as those at business-to-business (B2B) companies to say their companies' marketing metrics are very standardized.[26] The problem is that the more short term a company's focus becomes, the more likely the firm will demonstrate a tendency to engage in business behaviors that actually destroy long-term value. Once again, it is obvious that the obsession with current revenue and earnings has generated a pervasive culture of bad management, in which the customer value is nearly excluded. You don't create shareholder value by getting larger through acquisition but rather through organic growth. To do so, you must focus on your customers and know how to optimize your investments in order to create value for the clientele. To measure the ROI of their marketing investments, companies should use more than ROC (Return on customer). Enlarging your scope of measures is the only way to evaluate and strengthen your business—by creating maximum value from your scarcest resources. Peppers and Rogers define "return of customer" as the sum of a firm's current-period profits from its customers, plus any changes in customer equity (the sum of the lifetime values of all current and future customers served by the firm), divided by the total customer equity at the beginning of the period.[27] The argument underlying this approach is that the return on customer equals total shareholder return. Total shareholder return represents the change in capital value of a listed company over a period (typically at least one year), plus dividends, expressed as a percentage (plus or minus) of the operating value. It is a significant link between the customer satisfaction index (as a measure of perceived value by the customer) and the financial performance of a company at the corporate level. This relationship between customer value creation and shareholder value creation not only exists, but it is amplifying with the development of new economic realities linked to commoditization.

Customer-Centric Innovation: Mapping a Customer Job

Customers buy a product or a service to get a job done. This is why it is essential for companies to discover untapped jobs, that is to say problems customers are still facing without any satisfactory (commercial) solution at their disposal. The stronger the perceived importance of the job to be done, the greater will be the impact of the company's effort to find a solution, correlating to the height of a customer's sensitivity to the customized appeal the supplier will develop (as discussed in the previous chapter). Understanding what the customer values is fundamental, perhaps even more for the marketing function.[28] This understanding should not be restricted to marketing, however. Top executives should not rely on subordinates' reports to define and gauge the market, or they risk losing contact with the real world.

In terms of the customer value proposition, understanding the idea of a "job done" is easy, but identifying the job is a lot tougher. You need to be able to listen attentively to your potential customers as they describe their problems. You have to put yourself in their shoes and spend a day in their life.[29] Understanding their daily frustrations and difficulties is an excellent source of new product or service development in all markets. In an industrial context, the big difference is that you will have to determine who your real final customer is. A chemical company selling pesticides to farmers cannot count only on the differentiation of its latest chemical molecule. It needs the full support of major and local distributors and might also have to reach the farmers directly. Senior executives should consider the wants and needs of people at every stage of the distribution chain. This takes an innovative push-and-pull strategy. Strong CVPs should be used as push-and-pull drivers simultaneously along the distribution channel. The company must provide its wholesaler with adequate information and farmers with appropriate weather forecasts. In the field, a satellite-driven system, similar to a GPS, could guarantee fast delivery, especially in case of emergency.[30]

Customer value propositions that resonate with customers are very difficult to engineer. There is a reward, though. Once companies take a disciplined approach to understanding their customers, they can make smarter choices about where to allocate scarce resources. If you lack imagination or spontaneous creativity, consider importing practices from other industrial sectors or even other countries.[31] Innovation used to trickle down to developing markets from rich countries, but it has become a two-way street. Today, Nestle markets Maggi noodles—a low-cost South Asian hit—in Australia. Sending innovation managers abroad is a good way to hunt for inventions and new products associated with strong customer value propositions. HP uses its lab in India to research the migration of Web-interface applications for mobile phones in Asia and Africa to developed markets. GE learned to bring low-end products created specifically for emerging markets into wealthy markets, thereby disrupting itself.[32] Countries around the world are putting innovation at the top of their agenda. This trend is not exclusive to emergent economies. Companies have gained access to a global market for talent in many areas. An astute company will focus on countries where talents are suited to its activity and quest for innovative customer value propositions.[33]

A McKinsey global survey on business innovation found that although executives say innovation is very important, their companies' approach to it is often informal. Even worse, leaders lack confidence in their innovation decisions. Participants explained that quality and customer service are no longer differentiators, but rather prerequisites. Innovation is the best strategic decision for sustained competitive advantage. Close to 70 percent of corporate leaders said innovation is one of their top priorities, but less than 50 percent claimed that their decision process on innovation is well structured and managed. Only about one in four said it is driven by customer feedback! Sixty-seven percent of respondents said personal interactions with consumers are intended only to unearth the next new idea. Making innovation a core part of the executive agenda was reported by about half of all the respondents.[34] There is certainly room for improvement. It takes more than good intentions to innovate in a customer-centric way. Customers can lead you out of the commoditization trap, but real discipline is necessary at two levels. The first is the customer R&D strategy. The second is the approach itself—the way you generate ideas.

Regarding the customer R&D strategy, the more customer-centric you are, the longer it will take your competitors to figure out your game.[35] A successful customer R&D strategy requires companies to play both offense and defense. The offensive strategy is to establish a deep relationship with core customers, then extend the reach beyond the core, and eventually stretch into new customer realms. The defensive strategy involves continuously monitoring for shifts in needs and potential disruptive threats. One way to kill innovation is to isolate marketing, finance, and R&D and specifically to detach marketing from the customers. This disconnection is paradoxical, but it is common and might be caused by a dangerous tendency among marketing experts to think they know what consumers want. Keep in mind that marketing advances by appeasing customer rage. Focusing on sources of dissatisfaction is much more productive than gloating at sources of satisfaction. Saying that the causes of dissatisfaction are too numerous to be resolved is no excuse. The Pareto Principle (The 80/20 rule) generally applies. Discovering the very limited range of problems causing the large majority of complaints is easy. It is an excellent way to identify customer value propositions.

Now, let us focus on the approach. A semistructured approach can generate great ideas, even in familiar settings. The only thing you have to do is ask an organized set of concrete questions. For example, what do Rollerblades, Haagen-Dazs ice cream, and Spider-Man movies have in common? Each is something that adults loved as children and that was reproduced in an expensive form for grown-ups. Asking participants during a structured brainstorming to ponder how their childhood passions could be recast as adult offerings might generate fabulous ideas for new products or services.[36] Wild, outside-the-box approaches such as unstructured brainstorming do not work well because respondents are not very good at abstract reasoning. They get lost in the cosmos and need a basis for offering ideas and knowing whether they are making progress in the brainstorming session. Quantitative analysis doesn't give you a picture of the future: your respondents will focus on existing behaviors. Of course, you have to ask the right questions. A particular question that generates insights into a business is "What is the biggest hassle about using or buying our product or service?" Entrepreneurs who concentrate on eliminating hassles are generally successful: Jiffy Lube (on demand, fast-turnaround oil changes), for example, provides a pleasant environment at reasonable fixed prices. Prepaid phone cards are a good way to avoid unexpected high bills, especially for those with children who use cell phones. [Coyne, Clifford and Dye] provide a list of good questions. The first set is designed to "de-average" the customers (because they are not created equal and their needs differ). The second set explores unexpected success, for instance, use of a product or a service in ways the company never expected or intended. The third set looks beyond the boundaries of your business to understand the way different sectors have solved similar problems to yours. The fourth examines binding constraints, especially the biggest hassle arising from buying your product or service. The fifth set imagines perfection—what you could do with perfect access to information, for example. The sixth and last set revisits the premises underlying your processes and products, such as shifts in delivery or new trends in customers' needs.

You can also organize the questions according to the job (as a process) a customer is trying to get done. You need to map the different steps of the process, or produce a customer-centered innovation map.[40] The three steps in the definition process are as follows: (1) defining the execution step. What are the most central tasks involved in getting the job done?; (2) defining preexecution activities. What must be planned? What must be located or gathered? What must be prepared? What must be confirmed before execution?; (3) defining postexecution activities. What must be monitored or verified to ensure that the job has been done well? What must be modified or adjusted? What must be done to conclude the job and prepare the next one? Multiple innovation opportunities for making the customer's job easier or faster might arise at each step of this discrete process.

Rebuilding Trust? A New Socialist Perspective Applied to Business

Think of rebuilding trust and financial institutions immediately come to mind. Many people not only stopped believing our financial institutions were trustworthy but extended their disdain to many other companies in the broader economy.[37] Evidently, a modern economy can't function if people do not have faith that the institutions around them actually put their interests first.

Trust in institutions cannot be rebuilt until business leaders learn how to communicate honestly and create organizations where openness is the norm.[38] On top of that, executives have to realize that doing business is not only about money. Academicians believe that management education, especially at the MBA level, has not focused enough on what was previously called "values-based" leadership. Making profits has been the pillar of business education; ethical issues took a back seat. To dispel public distrust, business schools need to show that they value what society values.[39]

The key issue is that the revolution in online social media is radically changing what people value. Forget about state ownership, five-year-plan economies, or even total control by companies. A global collectivist society is coming, and whether people like it or not, they will have to adapt to it. A new socialism is surfacing.[40] It might be more successful than the old one because it has not been defined by politicians. It has emerged as a cultural movement based on the ideas of sharing, cooperation, collaboration, and collectivism. Do not believe the people who overreact and see this movement as a real threat. Bill Gates once derided open-source advocates with the worst epithet a capitalist can muster. These folks, he said, were "a new modern-day sort of communists," a malevolent force bent on destroying the monopolistic incentive that supports the American dream.[41] Was he ever wrong. The game of the "American dream" is over. The frantic global rush to connect everyone to everyone, anytime, anywhere, is quietly spawning a revised version of socialism that will have to be constructively integrated into business management. It is definitely not your grandfather's socialism.

Now I will explain how to promote a range of values through different approaches, with the help of technologies, in a global perspective, and consistent with the growing collectivism culture and its behavioral consequences. The scariest thing is that, despite the evidence of deceit, greed, and incompetence on a previously unimaginable scale, people still trust companies too much.[42] Sadly, some companies may take advantage of this weakness to perpetuate bad managerial practices. Instead of rebuilding (or rethinking) trust, another leitmotif in business management should prevail: putting values in value.

The Final Integrated Framework for Business Model Reinvention

Many challenging logics have been developed in the last few years. They are directly related to the subject of this book because all of them try to present new directions for developing fair and innovative creation of value for the customer. They reverse old, entrenched business paradigms and have assumptions in common. These logics are (1) the service-dominant logic of marketing, (2) effectuation as a new vision

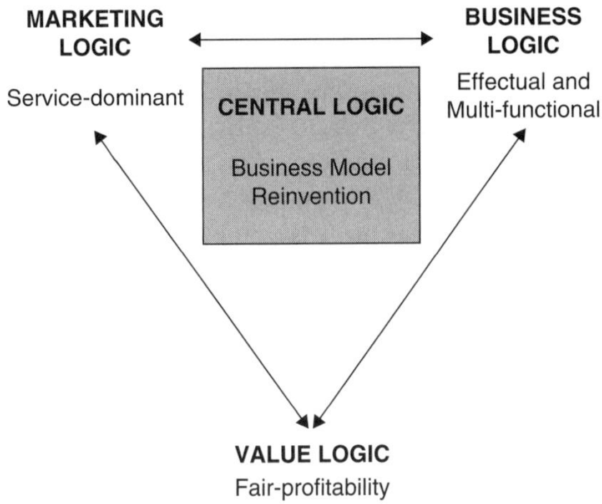

Figure 5.1 The final integration of new business logics.

of entrepreneurial expertise, and (3) the never-ending debate on the meaning of value.

In the following paragraphs, I integrate these views within a strong action-oriented perspective, with the reinvention of business models at its core (see figure 5.1).

The service-dominant logic of marketing is a challenging perspective for the marketing discipline.[43, 44] It is service oriented, customer oriented, relationship focused, and knowledge based. More importantly, marketing is considered a support function, central to the business strategy but not the pivotal function. Marketing shifts from a "market to" philosophy and business process in which customers are promoted to, targeted, and captured to a "market with" philosophy, in which customer and supply chain partners are collaborators in the entire marketing process. The service-dominant logic of marketing fits the philosophy of the reinvention of business models perfectly. The four Ps are cast aside definitively.[45]

Effectuation is a subtle, profound concept related to entrepreneurship, especially in a period of uncertainty, like the one existing now.[46] This view is challenging the nature of cause and effect in the social sciences. Its motto is: don't predict, invent the future! The principles and processes of the traditional predictive approach are the inverse of those of effectual approach. Predictive rationality rests on an underlying logic of foresight, the extent to which executives can predict the future. If prediction doesn't work, too bad. In contrast, effectuation rests on a logic of nonpredictive control; businesspeople do not need to predict the future. They just have to invent it. Executives initially bet on and invest in something they know how to do well and attempt to develop a directly related strong CVP, through cocreation with a network of partners, investors, and customer stakeholders. The resulting approach is naturally multifunctional.

Finally, the overall philosophy of integration should be guided by the willingness of companies to resolve a customer's problem, as explained earlier. Customer satisfaction and customer value creation are thus the driving objectives of the entire development process in a company, spanning all functions.

A new integrated model of action is taking shape. It should serve as the frame of reference for innovative reinvention of a business model. Change is pointless if it is not in the right direction.

CHAPTER 6

CVC Approaches: The Disruption Spectrum

> Progressive companies that create maximum value for their customers will survive and thrive; they will be able to carve sustainable competitive advantage in the marketplace.
>
> —William C. Johnson and Art Weinstein[1]

The previous chapter explained that the framework for business model reinvention is an integrated set of new business logics. I will now recommend ways executives can create value for their customers using this framework, with CVP as the backbone of all their activities.

Some very practical questions about the creation of value for customers naturally arise here. Reversing the stream of commoditization of commercial offerings by a balanced business approach that delivers equal benefits to the customer and the company is not easy. Few companies have successfully navigated these dangerous waters.

Our purpose here is not to show how fair pricing is nothing more than a collection of cognitive fallacies and biases about value.[2] It is not about field-tested tactics for engaging price shoppers and holding the line in declining profits.[3]

Of the strategic concerns that have often surfaced in discussions with executives, the first major one I will look at is how to determine which component of a commercial offering counts the most for the client. Do tangibles (products) outweigh intangibles (associated services)? How do you determine these relative weights? Case by case, by examining what makes the offer "discriminant" (really unique), or only determinant (responding to the needs, but no more), in your customers' view? It is important to distinguish between the short, medium, and long term because a discriminant offer often becomes only determinant, sometimes very quickly.

The second issue is whether innovation in creation of value for the customer differs between companies, particularly between an SME (Small and Medium Enterprise) and a multinational or between a company operating in a mass consumption sector and another in an industrial goods sector.

The third, and most complex, question is whether successful creation of value for customers invariably calls for extremely disruptive innovation or if it can also entail less radical changes or incremental innovation. In other words, can we make something new out of something old?

To answer these three fundamental questions about innovation in creation of value for the customer, it is crucial that the customers consider the experience of purchasing and using the product or service a success. Once again, this underlines the importance of service quality as the prime means of combating the perverse effects of the rise in perceived parity among a company's commercial offerings.

The underlying theme of this chapter is very simple. In business management, the most difficult to manage business processes allow the most talented company executives to stand out. However, the combined complexity of the global economy, market behavior, and new technologies makes these consequential business decisions more difficult than ever. Because it is harder for some companies to recognize and act on these processes, the quality of companies' commercial offerings varies considerably. Owing to the growing complexity of business management, success in business is becoming increasingly limited to a small number of companies with extraordinary leaders. Other exceptions are companies that operate in a monopoly situation or on a protected market. These conditions, however, are rare and may not last forever. It will be even harder for these companies to wake up if they have not given their customers due attention in the past. As soon as the customers have a choice, they will flee. Clients cannot be trapped—they must be earned!

I will answer the questions above and then list approaches to customer value creation based on degree of innovation. These approaches will be evaluated according to their capacity to propose solutions to customers' personal or professional problems and thus "get the job done."

Tangible/Intangible, Determinant Versus Discriminant

A positive and significant chain reaction at all levels of the organization affects everything from the quality of a commercial offering to that of financial performance, including customer satisfaction and market share. Within an appropriate field of action in each of these variables, the cause and effect are consistent: a plus leads to a plus and a minus creates a minus. This chain reaction is incontrovertible. It has been quantified, measured, and validated extensively in many sectors and countries. It is therefore not a theory detached from reality, as some executives claim. It is certainly possible to take its practical application too far and alter the chain effects. For example, investing in an extreme service offering (e.g., zero defects) can be excessive, as can chasing after a needless increase of a single point of market share when you already have a majority.

Databases such as ACSI (American Consumer Satisfaction Index, www.theacsi.org) show that the average satisfaction with products (all types) is markedly higher than satisfaction with services.[4] In addition, the average variance in satisfaction among companies follows the same trend: services companies find it harder to obtain satisfaction scores as high as those of manufacturers of tangible products such as durable goods. This implies that the perceived quality of products offered, both in industrial and durable goods, is relatively high on average. In fact, the overall quality of products has increased over the last few decades. In contrast, the quality of services has slumped considerably. It is not surprising that all the studies on this subject show that the main cause of a customer's choice to switch suppliers (manufacturer or distributor) is poor service. This proves that if the perceived parity of tangibles is very high, the only way to stand out is through service.

Take the case of car rental companies. They all have cars. The only difference is the particular brands available. A company could stand out by renting only Japanese cars, for example, but I don't know of any that do. They rent "cars," in other words, commodities. The rates are not very differentiated. What competitive lever is left? Certainly not the design of rental counters; they differ only in their color scheme. This leaves the quality of service provision. Has this "problem" been solved yet? Certainly not. Even at Avis, despite its slogan "We try harder!" (and they did, honestly) there is still room for improvement. Avis has to try even harder.

Companies must keep in mind that a major component of a customer value proposition is service quality. Service quality is not an expense but an investment! This has often been repeated but does not seem to have been understood or acted on, given the abysmal results of some satisfaction indices in the services sector. This does not mean that service excellence can make up the entire customer value proposition. Rather, it is a pillar of the business model that encompasses all the functions of the organization.

Granted, pursuing differentiation by developing innovations in services is often frustrating because services are easy to copy. It is important to make the distinction between discriminant and determinant. The former may quickly become the latter. When you offer something other companies do not, particularly a service, your offer is discriminant. It makes you unique and differentiates you strongly from your competitors, especially if your proposition is attractive. Inevitably, competitors will quickly copy you and offer the same advantage; they may even enhance it. Your offer will then lose its discriminant quality; your customers' advantage will simply become determinant. That is to say, you will no longer gain customers with this advantage. However, if you cut this service or product, you may see a sharp plunge in your customer volume and consequently your sales. Customers quickly learn to demand everywhere what they have received somewhere once, either from you or from someone else.

This perpetual race to gain a discriminant advantage, which quickly deteriorates into a determinant advantage, is exhausting. It demands endless research and constant innovation. At the same time, you have to watch your margins. If you aren't careful, you will end up offering "more" without equivalent monetary compensation. This will erode your profitability, a common occurrence in the business world. It all stems from hypercompetition: virtually unlimited choice that comes from globalization, intended for potential customers with almost infinite access to multiple purchase options (products, brands, and distribution circuits). Like it or not, investments in innovation must go hand in hand with cost control in development and operations.

Keep in mind that the more sophisticated the service, the harder it is to copy. At least it will take longer for competitors to do so. Service quality often rests on people and their attributes. Be particularly vigilant when hiring and training your staff. Some people should be kept at a distance from the customers, say in the back office, to avoid hampering customer relations. To understand customers' problems and come up with appropriate solutions, the staff must be caring, thoughtful, and good listeners. If not, the resulting conflicts would seriously tarnish the company's image and that of its entire staff. Customers' negative feelings reverberate throughout the image of the company concerned: this is called the halo effect. It is a nightmare scenario for all companies, especially service companies. They have to strive to make the quality of daily interaction with customers as pleasant and homogeneous as possible.

Innovation: A Universal Approach?

A very common complaint among business people is that advances in creation of value are applicable only to mass consumption products, as opposed to industrial products.

This view is quite alarming. It implies that people are thinking within airtight silos and believe that what goes on in different sectors has no bearing on their own situation. That is, many business people think that what is possible for consumer goods is not transferable to the industrial products. But this is a misconception that arises from the fact that they are not receptive to ideas coming from other sectors. In contrast, open-minded executives wonder whether what is possible in one sector could succeed in another. Why are some executives so obtuse that they refuse to examine other sectors and discover myriad new ideas? This compartmentalization mentality is so strong even within a group that two divisions of a large company may be resistant to meet and exchange ideas or creative approaches that could benefit the whole group.

Here is a rare positive example of the power of open-mindedness. In one of the executive development programs I gave, I had the honor of teaching high-potential engineers from Tata Steel. They were enrolled in a general program, not specific to their company. Their cohorts came from such diverse sectors as cosmetics, luxury products, banking, and pharmaceutical products. Most of the participants from Tata Steel were engineers and they were somewhat out of their element during the first sessions of my marketing courses. They found making the customers' perceptions a priority in engineering a difficult concept to grasp. It meant putting their perceptions above scientific rigor. In addition, examples about anti-aging cream or similar products went over their heads. But by the end of three two-week sessions, the engineers had mastered the marketing function better than participants from large companies who had bragged about their expertise in this area. Soon after they returned to India, they innovated by breaking all the rules in the industry. They applied marketing principles for mass consumption goods, particularly the famous concept of perceptual positioning (the positioning of products and services in the minds of customers), to industrial sales of steel, a commodity *par excellence*. They differentiated each line of steel, giving them individual brand names associated with a statement of value. Each line was thus positioned as a subbrand under the umbrella brand of the Tata Steel family. Each unique sales proposition was written directly for the target clientele. In taking this radical but necessary step, they exhibited outstanding guts, courage, and audacity. Success followed almost immediately. The guardians of marketing orthodoxy, the hardened conservatives, would say that this is not how to sell steel. In fact, this new approach works so well because it pleases the customers, who find it familiar. It also simultaneously targets the industrial and mass consumption markets.

The important lesson here is that creation of value for customers is universal. There is no need to partition approaches.[5] However, relationship marketing is better suited to the industrial world than to mass consumption products. Enlightened and clever competitors have figured out how to successfully ignore hard-and-fast rules. Misconceptions are also counterproductive. When commercial development of the Internet began, a large number of mistruths were said (and written): it would be a market of men only, yet the majority are women; companies wouldn't sell much clothing or shoes, but growth in these areas is among the strongest; it's just for young people, but retirees flock to the medium; and so on. Everyone agreed that the Internet posed a threat to selective products and an opportunity for mass products. Were they ever wrong! Selective products, particularly cosmetics, demand intensive relationship marketing. This is the ideal platform for the Internet. CRM (customer relationship management) has thus been transformed into e-CRM. It turns out that women express their intimate beauty problems more freely on cosmetics sites than they do with beauty consultants in stores. Rejecting a tool as innovative as the Internet offhand, as some cosmetics players did, and dismissing its potential for relationship marketing via a Web site is the best way to miss out on creating value for the customers (especially male customers). Fortunately, attitudes have changed, although for selective products the use of the Internet or Wi-Fi requires total control over the virtual distribution channel. It must remain the property of the company or commoditization will spiral.

Even the industrial world contains customers. The trick is to know how to deliver value by adjusting the mix of communication tools and distribution. All technologies are tools, not ends. The priority of creating value for the customer is therefore universal, as is the need to translate creation of value into a customer value proposition. Only the approaches vary, depending on the circumstances (types of products, sectors, geographical regions, etc.).

Above all, companies must not use these approaches to control customers rather than to try to improve service.[6] If they miss this point, all their approaches are doomed to fail. Using value creation tools, particularly relationship marketing tools, to wield control over the customers will inevitably lead to poor company performance. If, as an executive, you do not heed this warning, you have no right to complain that the approach used did not work. A bad carpenter always blames his tools.

Innovation: Incremental Only? Disruptive or Extreme?

If in recent years some radical innovations in business models have had undeniable impacts on the fortunes of some companies, more limited or incremental innovations have also made their mark. Without calling everything into question and rebuilding the organization from scratch, incremental innovations often allow companies of all sizes to maintain or improve income and profits.

In fact, the degree of innovation required for business success varies considerably. To ensure survival, growth, and profitability, and in response to mounting pressure from commoditization, companies must manage evolution gently via innovation rather than plunging into a "bloody" revolution. Both limited innovations and disruptive innovations can be successful. The important thing is for the approach to be suited to the circumstances and yield positive results in terms of company development.

However, when a company's business model is literally crumbling from decay, limited innovations will simply delay the decline and the closing down of business activities. In business, resuscitating a defunct model is a form of futile stalling. A poorly managed company can be revived, but you cannot breathe life into a business model that no longer meets the market conditions.

The same is true for a company as a whole. The simultaneous pursuit of incremental and disruptive innovation is an imperative. Innovation in creation of value for the customers resembles a pyramid.[7] The top contains a small number of major disruptions. The middle contains promising innovations. The base features a larger number of innovations with a more limited scope. They work best in conjunction with other innovations of the same type and thus gain efficiency and force to propel the company forward. Therefore, not all innovations need to be "blockbusters," that is, major and sweeping, calling into question nearly all of the dimensions of a business model.

Although chapter 4 portrayed the complete reinvention of a business model as the ideal solution to face the new economy, this total reconstruction is not within everyone's reach. Neither is it suitable for every situation. Just as a tanker cannot turn on a dime, one cannot expect a profitable company to completely and suddenly demolish its structure just to put in place a new business process based on new technology that suddenly becomes fashionable.

Not only do companies have to try to determine the innovations that would best serve the customer, but it is vital to affirm that such innovations will be assimilated and accepted within the company and its culture. P&G found it hard to integrate a relationship approach in its marketing practice. However, for years this large company has been considered a top reference in mass marketing, mainly because of its exclusive use of the traditional mass advertising approach. Although detergent sales do not lend themselves very well to development of a relationship marketing approach with customers, the company culture was also ill-prepared to make such a sharp turn. Its prestige, however, remains untarnished. Taken to the extreme, a violent rejection of a new approach to value creation could cause needless destruction. This may explain why many strong companies saw their financial results decline following the sudden and radical implementation of new CRM approaches.

At the base of the innovation pyramid, some strategic approaches are both innovative and classic. These two qualities are not necessarily contradictory. Simply put, a company can "innovate" by taking previously unexplored "classic" avenues. For instance, they can enter new domestic markets, target new segments, venture abroad, try out new product-market combinations, take advantage of the emergence of new markets, propose a new brand in response to increased sensitivity to price or to protect a star brand, and so on. These innovations are very classic and are formalized around known matrices such as Ansoff's diversification strategies: new or old products, new or old markets.[8] Nonetheless, this vision does not place priority on the quest for creation of value for the customer and will likely not lead to the formulation of an attractive proposition that resonates strongly with the customers.

To truly highlight CVC, it is important to identify the specific tools available, along with their real capacities and limits. You can then choose one or more tools suited to what you want to do and, more importantly, what you can do. A particular tool can be used singly or in combination with others. The notion of tools is vast, ranging from concepts, paradigms, and business processes to technologies and any other means to reach a specific end. The value of the outcome is measured by the customers first, rather than by the company.

Tools can be categorized. Some are more or less recent; some are disruptive or part of a classic tool kit the company can easily access. Companies should choose the most appropriate strategies to create an attractive customer proposition in the form of the much vaunted commercial solution to the customers' problems, depending on the circumstances and market conditions. What bears repeating is that none of these tools is exclusive. The best results are obtained by choosing one or more tools from among a panoply.

Below is a list of tools in the form of approaches to creation of value for the customers. It starts with tools that are more incremental and ends with those that are the most extreme. The most disruptive tools demand a total restructuring of the organization.

Customer Value Creation: A Review

Before I review the approaches to innovation, it is important to keep in mind that the goal here is to examine the extent to which each tool can contribute to creating value for the targeted customer. The approaches will not be analyzed in detail; readers who would like to know more about a particular approach should consult specialized publications or seminars.

Incremental Approaches

From Commodity to Cachet or Cult Branding (CVC by Brand Personality)

Can companies counter the relative and universal decline in the role of brands in the customers' decision-making process? If so, how? In the specific framework of value creation for the customer, the question of the potential role of a brand boils down to this: Can a brand be all or part of a solution to a customer's problem, whether the customer be an individual or an industrial buyer? Does the brand have a sufficiently strong personality to serve as a solution?

With the proliferation of brands on markets and the rise in perceived parity of brands by customers, all bets are off. If the brand is perceived primarily as a guarantee of quality, it solves a basic problem and becomes merely a benchmark. All brands, including distributors', should simply be of quality and especially be perceived as such by the customers to solve their basic problem. However, because many brands in a given product or service category are perceived by the clients as being of similar quality, the phenomenon of parity between offers is accentuated. Customers will seek plus (extra) value elsewhere, in another attribute that may be associated with another brand. Once again, differentiation can extend to the service surrounding the brand. This will be discussed below. The brand can also become a central point of reference for the solution to the customers' problem if its personality is strong enough to make it a cult brand.[9, 10] Acquiring and owning a cult product or service thus solves the customers' identification problems. For instance, it can boost social status (recognition because they own an exclusive, prestigious brand such as a Rolex watch) or serve an intellectual purpose because it uses different technologies (such as an Apple computer).[11] Other customers seek freedom at any price by opting for open-source rather than proprietary systems (as with avid Linux fans).

Unexpectedly, some executives tried to revitalize their companies by totally overhauling their product line, brand policies in particular. Even cash cows were slaughtered. Given this type of business approach, we can ask whether this is really creative destruction (and therefore positive) or a dangerous game similar to a sudden head butt by top management that amounts to the destruction of the company's brand capital and products. One example is PepsiCo., which initiated an upheaval in 2009.[12] Suddenly and brutally recasting your brand policies to face the new economy is very risky. You expose yourself to dramatic responses by your clientele. This is how the Merrill Lynch brand lost its cachet.[13]

To face pressure on brands, most large companies tend to consolidate their brand portfolio, which has more to do with sound cost management than with the will to create value for customers. In the case of Pepsi, the CEO demanded not only new advertising campaigns and new slogans for seven major brands, but also the reengineering of the design of over 1,000 bottles, cans, and packages. On top of that, it all had to be on the store shelves in seven months! Will this strategy allow the executive to achieve his goal of changing the rules of the market? I highly doubt it. First, exactly which rules is he intending to change? It is far from certain that these new rules, whatever they are, will provide new solutions for the customers.

As many experts in brand management assert, the personality of a brand counts. It's a way to preserve its authenticity and especially to ensure that the brand is present in all brands evoked by the customer (the limited set of brands considered by a customer for a purchase, or evoked set). Only cult brands will have a deep enough foundation to resonate with the customer, create a true relationship, and thus acquire a discriminant dimension in the brand choice process.

Without the potential to create a relationship with the customer, a brand cannot be the main driver of a customer value proposition. It can be the visual signature of a brand identity. It can define a territory. That's a good start. In short, not every brand is destined to become a cult brand, especially in highly commoditized sectors.

Top Customer Service (CVC by Customer Experience Management)

Clearly, service quality is an excellent way to make the customers' experience enjoyable, particularly by supplying solutions to their problems. It can even be a question of survival for a company because in the new economy, pleasing the customers is more critical than ever.[14, 15] Given the commoditization of offers (raw product or service), the creation of value has shifted to peripheral services. The determinant aspect of a choice criterion is central to the offer, whereas the discriminant aspects that make a huge difference in the way customers' (end or industrial) problems are solved lie in peripheral services.

Even if these peripheral services are ultimately copied by the competition, not every company can regularly deliver a quality service.[16] This skill, once acquired and honed, is not as easy to copy as some may think, fortunately. It is often the noninterchangeable quality of a company's staff that makes a company stands out in the way it helps customers solve their problems.

The service logic is now considered dominant in marketing.[17] Marketing experts, particularly academics, recognized and emphasized this fact only recently, which is surprising given that experts in other fields of business management have been advocating this view for a long time. The well-known service profit chain is a good example.[18] Part of a value-for-money perspective, this chain puts priority on employee satisfaction to foster customer satisfaction, which in turn drives commercial and financial performance. This service value corresponds precisely to the integration of business logics proposed at the end of the previous chapter.

Customization (CVC by CRM, e-CRM, and 121)

Using technology to turbocharge innovation during a period of economic difficulty can be a good strategy. History shows that radical economic changes, often associated with repeated crises, have fueled major advances in business management. The use of new technologies (hardware and software) must be sound, which means that it must not be dominated uniquely by an engineering logic but rather by a client logic, that is, by the company's willingness to share the technological benefits with its customers, particularly regarding creation of value. A company is more than just a playground for engineers. Executives must harness technologies to ensure that customer relations are user friendly.

Customization of commercial offers, or mass customization, is an undeniably valuable solution because it allows a company to configure its offers to customers' specific needs. It has high potential for being a strong and discriminant dimension in the customer value proposition. Examples include offering accounting software adapted to the needs of independent craftspeople, proposing specialized insurance for collectible cars, and offering gift wrapping on a Web site with an added option of writing a note to the recipient—all in response to specific needs of buying situations or types of purchase (for example, as a gift or personal). All these personalized services pay off. Often, the customer's price sensitivity decreases, for example, in an urgent situation (a last-minute gift) or because the need to receive a customized product takes precedence over other considerations. More extreme examples include designing customized racing bikes or producing shoes based on a 3D system, all at very high prices. Zappos.com offers its customers a vast choice of shoes in all sizes. If they don't have the model in stock, the online distributor will find it. Its prices are not particularly cheap, but the service is outstanding, especially for people who do not like spending time looking for shoes in their size in stores or who are simply too busy.

Customization is therefore the pillar of CRM. As part of CRM, information on customers must be gathered to supply the database and provide customers with appropriate solutions. The more the system learns about you, the more it can refine the offering. Executives must keep in mind that they are often sitting on a gold mine of opportunities: commercial solutions they can offer their own customers.[19]

Without fail, companies skid off course when they use data gathered to control customers, particularly by trying to differentiate good and bad customers—to identify those who generate profits for the company and those who drain them. They have missed the point of customer value creation. This is why a very large Canadian bank received disappointing scores in customer satisfaction among all its retail and business clienteles despite having one of the most sophisticated databases in the world. The problem lies in the internal culture, specifically top management's attitude toward the customers.

Further, "petabyte" marketing (based on the concept of the "personal petabyte," that says that the sums of all individual experiences will fit in a petabyte of information and stored in a petabyte-scale data warehouse) is taking the race for information that tracks the customer's slightest gestures and movements to the extreme.[20] Will the economic value of the information overshadow and even preclude the creation of useful and real value for the customer? This timely question deserves serious thought. Don't forget that CRM, by definition, entails sharing profits. If the company guarantees the customer a good purchasing experience, the customer will tend to be more loyal, in addition to being ready to pay more for it. This issue is indeed timely because the baby boomers, the engines of economy with their previously voracious consumption, have now developed an accentuated awareness of the family budget. They will continue to demand customer advantages but will be less carefree and are keeping a tighter hold on their wallets. It's a tough wake-up call for them. Companies must adapt to this reality and focus on Generations X and Y.[21, 22, 23]

Local Prevails Over Global (CVC by Adaptation)

During its conception and launch phases, market globalization (i.e., of marketing practices of large companies) rested on the attractive prospect of substantial economies of scale. It was believed that, by harmonizing needs throughout the world, globalization would lead all customers on the planet to demand the same products or services as solutions to their problems. Initially, the creation of value associated with a market globalization perspective had a predominantly financial slant. It aimed at reducing the unit costs of production, associated with a simultaneous narrowing of product lines. Sizeable gains in profits were foreseen, which would presumably be repatriated to the markets of origin of multinationals. As most of these large companies were American, it is not surprising that globalization was invented and wholeheartedly endorsed in the United States of America.

However, things didn't unfold exactly as planned. Today, everyone agrees that implementation of every strategy must be primarily local, even it originates within a global perspective.[24] The smoothing of needs—that is, the standardization of solutions provided to customers—was not as extensive as projected. Of course, commercial solutions to customers' problems are always more appropriate if they take into account local characteristics, including cultural aspects.

"Think global and act local" has become the motto of all companies operating internationally. This is the only way to achieve equilibrium between creation of value in a company (i.e., for its shareholders) and creation of value for customers around the world. It is a win-win formula in the adaptation of business solutions on a country-by-country basis.

To summarize, adaptation of business offerings to local conditions can generate substantial gains in creation of value for customers in export markets abroad. All the same, to reduce costs, companies can apply certain dimensions of business solutions across countries. Once again, flexibility is crucial in the quest for a fair balance between costs and efficiency.

Provocative Selling (CVC by Challenging)

No one can deny that selling products and services to industrial clients has become quite challenging. Although the idea of proposing solutions to their professional problems rather than proposing products and services is not new, it is still very relevant today.

What is new, however, is that the approach to proposing and selling these solutions must be more refined than ever. During negotiations with buyers, the seller's approach must be particularly well structured, even forceful. This does not imply aggressive argumentation, but it does mean not hesitating to challenge industrial buyers by daring to raise strong ideas that directly touch on the future of the company.[25] This approach does not negate the need to maintain a fair balance between the interests of suppliers and their clients.

First, salespeople's overly assured argumentation, which may be perceived as arrogant, is not necessary. Tight negotiations should cover each of the points considered important by the individual buyer or the unit in charge of purchasing. You have to prove to the customer that the characteristics of your offer are extraordinary and be able to credibly justify the price.

Second, when trying to convince industrial customers, salespeople may have to take the arguments into higher gear, by strengthening them and constructively provoking the customer. This entails trying to convince the customer to see things from your perspective and urging them to consider the major points of shocking arguments.

Of course, this audacious, forceful approach demands special training so salespeople can effectively make a provocative commercial argument with conviction. The ground rule is to maintain momentum in each of the phases of negotiation. This takes a lot of preparation. More professionalism than ever is needed to portray industrial goods as a unique, prized solution for the customers. The skills of the sales force make all the difference. Lastly, your sellers must have advanced technical skills, even engineering expertise. Simple sales talk is no longer enough.

The Disruptive Approaches

New Retail Business Models (CVC by Total Access)

All forms of distribution must be adapted to new market realities. Every distribution model is currently seeking new formats for its units (bricks) or Web sites (clicks). The recent changes, particularly in purchasing behaviors, have been so radical that if a distribution formula is not adapted, it will probably hit the wall.[26] At first glance, multichannel strategies seem to be in the spotlight. For instance, European hypermarkets are not necessarily the best solution to tight management of family budgets.

That being said, solutions must be proposed not only to loyal customers; companies must also seek out additional market share among disloyal or transitional customers.[27] This should not prevent you from reducing the gap between what you offer and what your customers want. While seeking out new clients, distributors and retailers must also give existing clients an additional reason not to stray. In distribution and retail trade, only "bad costs" should be cut: avoid cutting costs that directly affect the advantages you offer your customers.

Shopping on the Internet or any other digital platform is often an ideal solution to customers' major and stressful lifestyle constraints. Online shopping is an excellent solution for working women in particular. This obvious fact hasn't been fully exploited.[28]

Lastly, you have to identify the best strategic choices and most effective tactics between pure cyberplayers (clicks only), traditional stores (bricks), and hybrid formulas (bricks and clicks). Comparative evaluation must be done from the customer's perspective to pinpoint which channel, store format, or Web site architecture is the right solution for the customer.

For example, if a household wants to buy a family home and visits several units they find on the Internet, the broker hired would have to manage the visits to all these properties, regardless of which companies they represent. Financial transactions can be done directly from the broker's car, via a mobile digital system. In brokerage, this would create a "one-car" solution, based on the long-standing formula in traditional retail commerce in bricks and mortar of "all under one roof."

Reclining chair manufacturer La-Z-Boy quite astutely offered potential customers a chance to recreate the layout of their living room on its Web site to see how to place one of its products (location and color), using basic computer-assisted design software. This is how it enticed clients to its traditional (brick) store to purchase the item. The synergy between clicks and bricks is such that the conversion rate of customers entering the La-Z-Boy store and making a purchase is over 80 percent.

If you notice that, like Dell, your direct sales model no longer guarantees enough growth and that many people are reluctant to buy a computer on the Internet, it may be time to diversify your distribution policy, place your products in brick stores, and propose a solution acceptable to the customers who previously slipped through your grasp. This is a major strategic decision.

There are many other examples. Distribution in bricks or clicks is the meeting place between manufacturers and customers. It is only natural that this juncture undergo many changes, in sync with the rapidly evolving solutions for customers.

The Long Tail (CVC by Access to Rarity)

One innovative idea in commerce that has sparked much heated debate is the Long Tail.[29] Should companies focus exclusively on retail sales of star products, or blockbusters, or should they provide a specialized offering of rarer, niche products that are harder to find? Just as small streams lead to large rivers, supporters of the Long Tail approach confirm that sales of rare products can equal or even exceed those of star products in total value.

The debate is raging. Unfortunately, once again, the most virulent critics have not considered the customers' points of view, interests, or real wants.

The idea of the Long Tail is hot because it aims to create added value by the rarity of offerings rather than the quantity.[30, 31, 32] In short, something rare is not a commodity, unlike a product or service sold in millions of units. Thanks to new digital technologies and their growing capacity for data processing, companies can now help their customers track down or discover rare products and then sell them with a margin for the service rendered. This may entail cross-selling to help the customer delve further into a particular area. Search engines controlled by the manufacturer or distributor, or approaches such as "collaborative filtering" or "genome marketing," push customers along the tail: people who like product X may also like products Y, Z, and so forth.[33]

Solutions proposed to retail customers often fall into two opposite camps. The two extremes are embodied by Wal-Mart and Amazon.com. Evidently, customers won't find rare products, from food to crafts supplies to furniture, at a large mass distributor. If customers are seeking increasingly personalized solutions to their acute personal needs, managing rarity in retail trade is clearly a viable strategic option. If it turns the mass distribution world upside down, it is certainly for the better. It may be time to admit that customers have the right to access rarer products, and not simply blockbusters, as the only commercial solutions to their problems. From a customer-value-added perspective, the attacks on the Long Tail approach seem unwarranted. There is no reason for the market to be locked in.

This approach, which resembles an open philosophy of business management, is also reflected in the strategic choices of top management of manufacturers. They are shifting their attention from distribution to production. In the pharmaceutical sector, for example, Novartis stands out by investing in development of new drugs intended to provide solutions (i.e., cures) for rarer illnesses. It knows it can succeed in this area, and its primary goal is to help the patients.[34] Most of its competitors, in contrast, are obsessed with the quest for blockbusters. This philosophy may even unsettle top management of some large companies. In 2009, the American pharmaceutical giant Pfizer suddenly proposed to deliver some of its drugs to the unemployed for free. Could this be their way of burnishing their image after creating astronomical monetary value?

In mass distribution of electronic products, Best Buy adopted a micro approach to its clientele and targeted particular niches, thus facilitating sales of blockbuster products.[35] Even in a niche market, companies can find effective commercial solutions.

Technological Convergence (CVC by New Solutions)

Convergence has become a catchall concept. This far-reaching phenomenon has affected technologies, communications (support and content), and applications. The basic idea is to ensure that resources of all kinds, initially with isolated operating modes, can exchange with and complement each other, be juxtaposed, and be used simultaneously as companies seek synergies and create new technical possibilities to provide new commercial solutions to customers. Technological convergence is thus triggering profound changes in customers' behavior.

For example, convergence between the world of computers and telephones has literally changed the landscape of these two industries, which have had to adapt to developments in online communication. The classic telephone was quickly replaced by Voice over Internet Protocol (VoIP). New telephony solutions were offered to customers, who quickly adopted them. These new, more advantageous formulas for customers forced classic telephone companies (AT&T in the United States of America, France Telecom, etc.) to reconfigure or perish. Knowing how to innovate in business and taking into account technological convergence is quite challenging. The first step might be to understand that convergence, by definition, follows divergence and that it is difficult to converge without having diverged.[36] Often, very simple technologies like MP3 facilitate convergence. The Skype explosion is one example, with its offering of cheap telephone calling via the Internet.[37]

In general, the more technological convergence leads to clear solutions for the customers, especially that in which practical implications are easy to grasp, the quicker and more easily it will be implemented and diffused. Customers must perceive all the advantages, including monetary. For example, customers can easily understand the current convergence between telephones and GPS systems. They see a practical way to make travel easier via a single support—their mobile phone. Customers are quickly adopting this new solution and modifying their lifestyle and consumption habits. It's that simple. This is why it is not surprising to see a leading company like Google putting a huge effort into simultaneously proposing, on the mobile GPS market, both its iPhone-style telephone (Android) and access to its Google Earth software adapted to this format. The software leads; the hardware follows. Now that Google has its own mobile platform, it only has to manage the content (travel and communication). The strategic idea behind this combined offer is to control access to information on people's actions and movements. The potential commercial benefits are huge and apparent; the people monitored are all potential customers.

Marketing X.0 (CVC by Getting Social Communities Right)

Marketing X.0 refers to all marketing approaches intended to create value for the customer via the Web (wireless or other), along with their evolution (2.0 and higher).[38]

The central question is how one best manages virtual communities to discover market opportunities in the form of appropriate commercial solutions that can then be proposed to the customers targeted by the offering of products or services (marketing studies). How can companies develop prototypes by connecting to virtual networks (R&D)? The last concern is how commercialization on these virtual markets should be carried out. For example, a company can begin by conducting marketing research on blogs, followed by participative innovation on a Web site by soliciting active customers (crowd-sourcing with prosumers), and then use applications like WiMax (a wireless broadband access technology) to geographically locate customers and help them find the solutions to their problems (geo-marketing). This approach can apply to a simple pizzeria downtown (WiMax) or to an overseas distributor of highly specialized industrial products (search engines on the Internet).

Companies are clearly finding it difficult to control virtual communities. The members of virtual communities are more interested in the social ties that can flow from affiliations with brands than in the brands themselves.[39] As a result, managing a community around a traditional brand, such as Harley-Davidson bikers, is not transposable as such in a virtual world. Within virtual communities, it is difficult to push the sale of products and services directly, even if you present them as good solutions to get the customer's job done. All the same, it is possible to extend your customers' positive experience via the media and social networks, particularly in real time.[40]

Some companies are betting heavily on real-time Web applications like Twitter or Facebook.[41] Here again, the initial motivations may contradict the internal values of virtual communities. Companies are trying hard to plumb virtual communities for "leads" that will let them push products and services on customers.[42] The sites that host these communities face a serious dilemma: they can reap profits by allowing commercial exploitation of the large quantity of member profiles and messages exchanged. This material can be dissected within a data mining approach to boost clients' sales. The problem is that the members of virtual communities are becoming increasingly opposed to shady business practices. Companies are trying to monetize social networks, and the old demons of high-pressure sales and short-term profit seeking are coming out of the woodwork.

Most companies still rely on traditional R&D infrastructures, in bricks and mortar, thinking that innovation must mainly be housed within their walls. A minority has understood that creation and development of new products and services, as solutions recognized by customers, should be compatible with social networks, according to a Wiki approach that is to say a collaborative approach, possibly located on a Web site, for compiling and integrating information, resources, competencies, and feedbacks coming for different sources.[43] Frontrunners such as P&G and Lego[44, 45] are going from R&D to C&D (connect-and-develop).[46] Some companies are data mining blog content to gather information. The Internet is thus transformed into a gigantic focus group in which customers discuss new products and trends. Cisco, Sprint, and Electronic Arts have adopted this approach, which requires developing software to analyze the content of discussions on blogs or message exchange sites.

Commercial practices related to direct management of virtual communities remain limited. Some companies join (more or less covertly) exchanges between members of virtual communities to promote the positive experiences of their existing customers among potential customers. Infiltrating virtual communities has become a business obsession. This relentless pursuit is easy to explain: executives who ceded power to their customers are now intent on recovering it at all costs, especially because virtual communities are a commercial gold mine. However, the fierce resistance of members of these communities is increasing the pressure.

Certainly, marketing X.0 practices may vary considerably between countries. The Japanese are quite accustomed to companies permanently following them on an individual basis to offer commercial solutions specific to their location (geographical dimension) and the time of day. Although technically WiMax technology can operate anywhere in the world, its implementation is not feasible in all countries.[47] Some countries are very advanced (Japan and Korea), whereas others lag behind and may even resist stubbornly (old Europe). The Americans are embracing this technology because the economic crisis is favoring all approaches that revitalize consumption.

The Extreme Approaches

Joining the Opposite Camp—The Case of Massive P2P (CVC by Embracing BitTorrent)

Direct exchanges of files between individuals, along with products and services via platforms such as eBay.com or alibaba.com, have grown to epic proportions. The P2P (peer-to-peer) economy has revolutionized the business world.[48] The snag is that, by definition, these exchanges are totally beyond the control of manufacturers or service companies, for the greater good of individuals who do not have to pay manufacturing rights such as copyright nor for the large margins often associated with certain kinds of products or services.

Consumers perceive these exchanges as a very practical solution. This massive popular rallying is driving a form of "e-barter" on the Internet.

For companies, the problem is aggravated by software that allows users to quickly and easily exchange large files. The evocatively named BitTorrent software, developed by a computer whiz, is one such application that has caused upheaval in both the music and film industries.

P2P adepts see this software as a miracle solution. Everyone knows that the faster the Internet connection, the quicker the downloading and the more people will use this connection, particularly for commercial transactions, including P2P. For the music and film majors (the largest companies in the industry), however, this software was a nightmare until the threat was transformed into a proprietary method of online film distribution. Rather than hopelessly and endlessly combating this new technology, Warner Brothers decided to acquire it and use it to distribute its films on the Internet.[49]

A solution that pleases the customers and gives them significant advantages should be repatriated by the company and reintegrated in its own production and distribution activities. This is much better than wasting energy and time trying to eliminate an elusive and uncontrollable threat. Some technologies are like tsunamis: their force is so strong that it can't be stopped. At best, it can be harnessed.

Blue Ocean Strategy (CVC by Changing the Rules of the Game)

The Blue Ocean Strategy is a key approach to creation of value.[50] In a nutshell, this method consists of radically changing the competitive framework of a company from an ocean of fierce competition (red) to a tranquil sea (blue).

Combining the analytical and the strategic, this method entails analyzing and painting a strategic portrait of a traditional sector around its dimensions. Strategic innovation then serves to almost fully reverse the profile of the business sector, related to nearly all the dimensions inventoried and a few new dimensions.

Take the international wine market. Traditionally, there were two main types of wines: premium and budget. Based on traditional dimensions such as age, the use of a specific wine appreciation terminology, the complexity of the vintage, and the nobility and prestige of the region of origin, it was possible to clearly demarcate profiles associated with the two main types of wines. The problem was that in markets with fewer connoisseurs, this demarcation was fully grasped by only a small minority of the customers.

Some producers then hatched the idea of breaking all the timeless conventions of the wine market and proposing a new profile, which does not follow tradition but has the advantage of delivering the benefits sought by a mass clientele; it was a simple solution. Some see this as outright pandering to the customers. New dimensions—presented as new attributes of the offering and therefore as new sales arguments—were put forth: easy to drink, simpler selection, more fun and adventure! You can practically hear traditional sommeliers and producers gnashing their teeth. Yellow Tail, an Australian wine, uncorked the American wine market by radically changing the face of the industry. Customers found, in this brand, the ideal solution to their problem of how to choose a wine. Incidentally, this wine is also available in France, at a specialized distribution chain. Who could have imagined?

When companies change the face of an entire competitive sector and pioneer an offering whose profile is perfectly adapted to the advantages sought by most customers, it is difficult for competitors to copy the product. This radical strategy of creation of (new) value for the customer allows companies to acquire a position of strength and a moment to catch their breath before the competitors rush in.

That said, even if the commercial marketing formula is a good one, competitors will eventually arrive. To return to the case of Yellow Tail, the market is now invaded by "exotic" wines of all kinds, a bustling menagerie of monkeys, kangaroos, cheetahs, gazelles, and so on. The blue ocean has again turned red because of the advent of the brand safari! The customers may then wonder whether the offering is more about the safari experience than the sampling of a fine wine.

Final Word on Creation of Value

I will close this last chapter of arguments before the conclusion by presenting two key ideas on customer value creation that summarize everything I have presented so far. These two ideas apply to business practice in general and to marketing in particular.

The first is that innovation has no "value" unless it truly provides value to the customer and the customer perceives this. To be effective, creation of value for the customer must be part of a "win-win" approach. The customers will be happy, and the company will guarantee its financial survival. For instance, it may be premature to claim that "sustainability" (meeting the needs of customers today without compromising those of the future) is the actual engine of innovation. This will depend on whether the customer feels the problem, makes it a priority, and sees your offerings as a valid solution to this problem.[51]

The second idea is linked to the first but has deeper ramifications. All the approaches we reviewed in this volume have been developed to serve the business world first, with the main proviso that each company should share all the benefits with the customers—except one.

The exception is virtual communities. These networks have not arisen to serve companies. They have succeeded precisely because they allow individuals to communicate freely with their peers without corporate interference. If, dazzled by the enormous commercial potential these communities represent, companies channel all their efforts into trying to "manage" them for their own purposes, they have a tough road ahead. They and their executives need to understand that these communities are vastly different from traditional brand communities. In virtual communities, individuals are in control, not companies. Resistance to companies' efforts to seize control will be fierce.

That is why business managers must grasp and accept the wikification of the global economy and its consequences on business management. This will be one of the main subjects of the following section, the conclusion of the book.

Conclusion

> I told everyone, be afraid of our customers, because they are the folks who have the money. Our competitors are never going to send us money.
>
> —Jeff Bezos[1]

Don't forget...

> The customer signs your paycheck.
>
> —Frank Cooper[2]

To deliver value to the customer...

> First build your wave, then ride it.
>
> —Jean-Claude Larréché[3]

This conclusion reviews the main ideas discussed here. I will also highlight the underlying intellectual process for the last time, to reinforce its validity. I go beyond summarizing the contents of this book and underline the main practical implications of all the arguments presented herein, particularly the perpetual reinvention of business models, the internal functioning modes of businesses, and leadership in business.

Undoubtedly, the topic of new leadership profiles alone deserves its own book. Publications on the need for renewed leadership in businesses have mushroomed in the months preceding this publication. I have not discussed this subject in depth for two reasons: it is not the focus of this book, and it falls into a different domain of expertise (human resources). However, I will underscore the important leadership issues that are directly linked to the need for customer value creation, business model reinvention, and business innovation.

The Market Economy: Not So "Irrational"

The severity of the latest economic crisis has prompted diverse experts, from economists and journalists specializing in market economics to businesspeople, to examine what went wrong. They are trying to find explanations for how the crisis changed the business landscape and to what extent.

Because the main economic models failed to rationally explain market behavior, these experts argued that the old models must be replaced with new, more powerful, and especially more reliable ones.[4] Undeniably, economists were unable to anticipate the amplitude of the changes that gripped market economies. To their credit, the economists had not seen a true seismic shift since 1929. It is only during periods of upheaval that experts can truly learn and identify the forces underlying the radical transformation of business landscapes. In this case, the major force was commoditization, the effects of which on the behavior of companies worldwide have been largely underestimated. Even financial models have been affected.[5] In short, the "modern" economic theory is a misnomer.

Insisting categorically, with perfect hindsight (only after the markets have collapsed), that the catastrophe was not foreseeable is definitely a form of intellectual hypocrisy. It seems like a defensive reaction by experts (in economics, business, etc.) caught off guard. The real problem is that the majority of the global business and economic community did not want to face the economic phenomena of recent years and heed the tiny minority of experts who had sounded the alarm.

The claim by other experts in business economics that the "rational economy" is dead is also questionable.[6] Economic models that supposedly represent market behavior are certainly rational. They have always been, although they purportedly model the behavior of markets and therefore individuals, who are irrational by nature. Human beings are subjective and don't act like machines, nor do they follow scientific rigor. The word "irrational" does not mean the behaviors in question lack meaning or logic. Business, consumption, and purchasing behaviors are conditioned by individuals' perceptions. They are not dictated by scientific dogma, which may certainly have a rigorous internal logic but may be disconnected from everyday reality.

More seriously, the latest crisis marks the rise and decline of the power of finance, associated with the demise of a society led solely by companies.[7] The myth of shareholder capitalism is over.[8]

The starting point for this book is the basic argument that the global economic crisis that erupted in 2008 was not an isolated event. There were repeated crises before, and there will be others. Asking whether the crisis is really over is not the right question, although it is certainly understandable from a human standpoint. During difficult times, everyone wants to turn the page. But a more in-depth understanding of recent events should change business economics experts' perspectives and help them adopt a long-term forward vision.

As Pres. Bill Clinton said, you have to create value even in a crisis. He recommended banking on the green economy, which he considered the next sector of major growth.[9] It's a very good idea, but it is only a partial solution because the current economic transformations are still profound. They encompass ecology but extend further. One of the main ideas in this book is that the series of recent crises are the tip of an iceberg. Beneath the surface lies the commoditization of business offerings. Commoditization may have been partly fueled by market globalization[10] but not entirely. The combined effect of globalization (multiplication of offerings) and digitization (multiplication of niches) has quickly led to the commoditization of new products and services and their very quick introduction in price markets. The lifespan of "specialty" products is shrinking quickly, as are companies' margins. It is not just individuals who burn out—companies do, too. The commoditization trap lies with the acceleration trap.[11] When margins erode, they deprive companies of breathing room. Companies have reacted to this constraining situation in various ways. Some struggle haphazardly, frantically cutting both good and bad costs. Others have tried to trim only the bad costs while creating customer value. Naturally, only the companies that create value and control costs simultaneously can resist the tide of commoditization. These executives have understood that low-cost models also imply high value as part of a winning formula: "low-cost/high-value" business models. Unfortunately, many executives focus only on the "low-cost" aspect of these models. This omission has a devastating effect because it fosters extreme business behaviors that amount to executives sawing the branch on which they are sitting.

This book puts the commoditization phenomenon under the microscope because executives who do not fully grasp this intricate process cannot envision solutions to ward off undesirable effects and survive. The previous chapters laid out an economic analysis, followed by solutions and strategic recommendations in the form of leads, using concrete examples. After reading this book, executives should be motivated to change their approach by acting not only on the economic analysis presented but also on the diagnosis of commoditization and the strategic recommendations for creation of customer value presented earlier in this book. In confronting the new economic reality and in accelerating corporate transformation, you must not lose your nerve![12]

Why Reinvent Business Models?

To create value, first we must agree on what the word "value" means and then find the factors that can create value most effectively.

This book emphasizes the primacy of the customer value proposition. The reward that follows is value for shareholders. Short-term profit seeking should never be the ultimate goal of business management. Nor should blind, systematic cost cutting. A more responsible business approach is needed as part of a fair and balanced value-for-money perspective.

That being said, what powers "healthy" corporate growth, and therefore deserved growth on stock markets, is an innovative business model. This holistic vision of the company encompasses the innovativeness of its products and its business process, along with management of the customer's experience.

This approach to business is thus multifunctional. It is oriented toward concrete realization of a strong customer value proposition that lets the company "get the job done." It provides real solutions to customers' personal or professional problems. The company's four Cs—coordination, cooperation, capability, and connection[13]—come into play rather than the four Ps of marketing. The next step is to seek synergies. For example, using the Internet as an entry platform in a virtual world must be combined with a physical Internet, real logistics that support the online purchasing activities.[14] By coordinating the consumers' end-to-end experience, companies could enjoy revenue increases of 10 to 20 percent.[15] To successfully manage all the connections within companies and the search for synergies, with the customer value proposition at its center, companies need to reinvent management and stoke dissatisfaction with the status quo.[16] Large companies such as GE are trying to make the search for growth part of the company's DNA. They want the company to function like an innovative team.[17] And GE dares (with courage) to disrupt itself: for decades, GE has sold modified Western products to emerging markets. Now the company is doing the reverse.[18]

Combating laziness is essential: employees' hearts and minds must be engaged.[19] Grasping for salvation is not a good solution,[20] especially because the notion of reinvention of business models is causing many executives to drag their feet. They don't want to go back to being entrepreneurs. Redesigning both the rationale of the company and its operating mode from scratch is quite a challenge. Understandably, some may give up. All the same, constant and radical evolution has become a market imperative for businesses. Executives at companies like Samsung are deliberately trying to create a perpetual climate of tension in their teams and make their company a potential crisis machine.[21] Employees may feel more stressed, but the system seems to work—for now. But how long can they keep up this pace without collapsing?

Although some companies let the business environment shape their structures and operating modes, a handful of others are cobbling together strategies that define their business environment.[22] Regardless of whether the approach followed is more or less extreme or disruptive, your business model must be perfectly aligned with the delivery of a strong CVP and must meet the expectations of all the company's partners. This is what I call the final collage around the customer value proposition.

New Leaders Wanted

Because business management must evolve to such a great extent, do today's leaders need the same profile as their precursors of two decades ago? Of course not!

Several corporate success factors have changed dramatically since the end of the last century. Two of these factors affect business management considerably: the need to accept customers' power and the need to open the company's territory, referred to earlier as "wikification."

These two factors make it very difficult to imagine the reactions of the big bosses of the past, who were so attached to the total closure of their company's territory and who found it inconceivable that a customer could tell them how to manage their company. Businesses' engagement in participative networks; the creation of open platforms accessible to competitors; openness to participative collaboration by customers, particularly in R&D and advertising creation; delegation of decision making to the local level; and many other open approaches would certainly be foreign concepts to these executives, not only because of their personality traits but also because of their notorious iron grip on the reins of their company.[23]

For leaders of conventional companies, taking the leap from a proprietary business management system to an open system is almost unthinkable. Traditional leaders would never willingly cede even partial control over their companies. They view Jeff Bezos, the emblematic head of Amazon.com, as an alien from another planet. All the same, Mr. Bezos is successfully countering commoditization and earning comfortable margins.[24] This quantum leap in perspective amounts to going from a totalitarian approach (albeit unconscious) to a more collaborative management approach. It may be too much for old-school executives to swallow. The leaders of the past cannot even imagine that open management could give their company a competitive lever that would be a potential source of growth and income.

Not surprisingly, this subject is being hotly debated among left-brain thinkers (good managers with a strong sense of structure but lacking imagination) and their right-brain counterparts (more imaginative but perhaps more disorganized).[25] This debate has even entered the boardroom.[26]

Clearly, given the rapid and complex evolution of new technologies, coupled with the need to respond to hypercompetition caused by globalization, leaders must be able to respond to new realities on a daily basis (formerly not the case). They must protect the business culture while continuing to believe in the future.[27, 28] While the storm rages unrelentingly, knowing how to keep a steady course and manage ambiguity and uncertainty have become more important leadership skills than ever.[29]

Finding executives who can foster the ongoing adaptation of their businesses, enduring discomfort and imbalances caused by constant changes while letting their employees experiment, is certainly not easy.[30] Some human resources experts have argued that emerging countries may be the ideal place to find leaders with extraordinary abilities to manage profound economic changes and repeated crises,[31] who seem to be in short supply in the West. The reason is simple: more and more technological disruptions come from these countries, and their economic conditions dictate that these companies integrate low-cost/high-value approaches in their business models. Leaders from emerging countries are immersed in a culture that teaches them, from birth, to surf the wave of commoditization.

It is certainly not the leaders who thrive on paperwork and the meeting culture who will have the right profiles to combat commoditization. Companies will have to allow frontline managers to realize their full potential rather than stifling them with internal constraints that inhibit their ability to adapt in the field.[32]

To summarize, leaders must update their cognitive maps if they are to change the way their businesses function. This change is so massive that a new concept of leadership has become an urgent priority.[33]

Believe in Customer Satisfaction or Get Out!

There have always been executives who have not paid attention to their customers. Repeating endlessly in business publications and meetings that the customer is king does not mean that all executives have moved from words to action—far from it.

What is more surprising is that the growing pressure of commoditization on companies and therefore on the shoulders of business executives has not led the offenders to change their attitudes toward the customers.

Some people exhibit an extreme response. Their negative vision of the customer is powering an uncontrollable and systematic skid toward all customers (actual or potential) combined with a profound overt negativism, expressed particularly within the company. Employees are being told to try to trap the customers and focus exclusively on the company's short-term survival. Positive results must be delivered to shareholders at all costs over the short term, simply to allow the company to keep going, if only for another quarter. Our role, an executive of an ailing French bank confided, is to plug the gaps, daily; the customer is the least of our worries. We are trying to find ways to charge more service fees and generate income for our institution, he admitted.

Such extreme and destructive attitudes prompt ill-timed, vulgar, and unethical statements and actions toward the customers. These business behaviors are unjustifiable and unspeakable.

The regulation of capitalism does not apply solely to dubious practices of financial institutions. It should oblige every company to assume its social responsibilities and favor ethical business practices.

Once again, new business models must take into account all the company's partners—not only shareholders but especially customers and employees.[34] Understanding the key strategic role of the customer's experience is more vital than ever.[35, 36] Companies' long-term survival hangs in the balance. To adapt, companies need rigor and patience.[37] Managing customers is not easy, especially because the clientele is now in the driver's seat and they know it. This is why it is better to adapt to the new market situation.[38] Some large companies like P&G have done this very well. Determining the best solutions for customers is the top priority.

Always Map Your Competitive Advantage

The business approach underlined in this book is based on a philosophy of sharing the benefits with the customers, known as the value-for-money business perspective. Executives must always ensure that their company is fulfilling this essential function.

Often, when executives are asked to situate their company's position regarding the ratio of benefits to the sale price, they become quite confused.[39]

This question, however, is a fundamental one for all companies because it refers to the company's competitiveness from a low-cost/high-value perspective. As already mentioned, this perspective predominates on global markets and shows no sign of fading away.

A simple, effective way to perform this assessment is to map your competitive position along two axes: plot the added value of your offering on the X axis and the distribution of your sale price (yours and those of your competitors) on the Y axis. This tool goes far beyond traditional marketing analysis because it provides a strategic vision of your competitive position under current market conditions.

Lastly, when assessing competing propositions on a given market, you may be surprised to learn that the customer's experiences during purchases sometimes count for more than the actual product or service. Make no mistake: this is one of the concrete manifestations of commoditization of commercial propositions. It is up to you to adapt your strategic plan so that your company can take advantage of this situation.

Put Strategy Back Into Leadership and Restore Marketing to Its Rightful Place!

In 1997, Brandenburger and Nalebuff succinctly depicted the concept of value as the difference in the world with or without your company.

This difference corresponds to the specific added value of your business.[40]

Since then, general business strategy has changed dramatically. The main evolution concerns the central objective pursued by the management committee of the company when it defines the company's corporate strategy. Before the arrival of globalization and digitization (which jointly fueled commoditization), the central objective was to define a long-term sustainable competitive advantage. Today it is to create value. This means approaches to attain the corporate central objective have also evolved from formulation of a rigid plan resulting from an analytical exercise (left brain) to an adaptable, holistic, open, organic process. Prolonged implementation and execution phases have given way to ongoing daily strategizing.

Even though strategic activities must be performed daily, they are far from being mere tactics. Thinking this way would be very dangerous. Just because the time frame of strategic planning has shrunken considerably, this does not mean business management has been reduced to a series of stopgap measures.

This may seem paradoxical, but today there is a pressing need for "daily" management of long-term strategy. It's an art form. Unfortunately, short-term preoccupations and practices tend to outweigh a long-term vision, creating economic catastrophes.

What is the role of marketing here? As mentioned earlier, it must take its rightful place in the company. Not surprisingly, the four Ps have been affected by the crisis—marketing manages relations between companies and their customers, particularly related to communication and distribution. Because creation of a customer value proposition is central to the reinvention of the business model and the collage of the companies' operations, functions, and business processes, marketing evidently plays a major role in this process. It must take on a more strategic overall scope rather than be limited to simple management of integrated activities around the positioning of the four Ps. However, the strategic, renewed importance of marketing should not translate into exaggerated pride that drives marketing experts to make their function the most important one in the company. It isn't, and neither is the finance function. Any debate over absolute leadership is not only sterile but contrary to the company's interests, internal functioning, and overall market performance.

If there is one message to keep in mind after you put this book down, it is that a company is a set of egalitarian functions working toward the attainment of a common objective: customer value creation via a unique commercial proposition. Value is the benefit perceived by the customer. The collage implies that all functions contribute together, in their own way and on an equal basis, to delivering value to the customer as promised. The remuneration is fair profitability for the exchange of benefits between the customer, the company, the employees, and the shareholders. The ultimate performance indicator is the satisfaction the customer expresses. "Good" profits will then follow as a well-deserved reward.

NOTES

Introduction: All You Need Is C(l)ash

1. *BusinessWeek* (2009), "What Falling Prices Tell Us," February 16, 3p.
2. Olson, Matthews S., Derek von Bever, and Seth Verry (2008), "When Growth Stalls," *Harvard Business Review,* March, 15p (First-place Winner of the 50th Annual McKinsey Award).
3. Kim, Chan W. and R. Mauborgne (2004), *Blue Ocean Strategy,* Harvard Business School Press Book, December, 1st edition, 272p.
4. Foster, Richard (2008), "Creative Destruction and the Financial Crisis: An Interview with Richard Foster," *The McKinsey Quarterly*, December, 5p.
5. *BusinessWeek* (2002), "Can Sony Regain the Magic?" Cover Story, March 11, 72–80p.
6. Plantes, Mary Kay and Robert D. Finfrock (2008), *Beyond Price*, Greenleaf Book Group Press, 26p.
7. Kotler, Philip (2008), *Kotler Marketing Group*, www.kotlermarketing.com, Open Citation, a key idea fully developed in the Q/A part of his Web site.
8. Johnson, Mark, W. Clayton, M. Christensen, and Henning Kagermann (2008), "Reinventing Your Business Model," *Harvard Business Review*, December, 12p (Second-place Winner of the 50th Annual McKinsey Awards).
9. Foster, Richard (2008), "Creative Destruction and the Financial Crisis: An Interview with Richard Foster," *The McKinsey Quarterly*, December, 5p.
10. Margolis, Joshua D. And Paul G. Stoltz (2010), "How to Bounce Back from Adversity," *Harvard Business Review,* January–February, 7p.
11. Rust, Roland T., Christine Moorman, and Gaurav Bhalla (2010), "Rethinking Marketing," *Harvard Business Review,* January–February, 8p.
12. Collis, David and Michael G. Ruksyad (2008), "Can You Say What Your Strategy Is?" *Harvard Business Review,* April, 11p (First-place Winner—Tie—of the 50th Annual McKinsey Awards).
13. Jarvis, Jeff (2009), *What Would Google Do?* Collins Business, Harper Business Publishers,1st edition, 272p.

14. Christensen, Clayton M., Stephen P. Kaufman, and Willy C. Shik (2008), "Innovation Killers: How Financial Tools Destroy Your Capacity to Do New Things," *Harvard Business Review*, January, 8p.
15. Bonini, Sheila and Hans-Werner Kaas (2010), "Building a Sustainable Ford Motor Company: An Interview with Bill Ford," *The McKinsey Quarterly*, January, 10p.
16. Johnson, Mark, W. Clayton, M. Christensen, and Henning Kagermann (2008), "Reinventing Your Business Model," *Harvard Business Review*, December, 12p (Second- place Winner of the 50th Annual McKinsey Awards).
17. Holmes, Andrew (2008), *Commoditization and the Strategic Response*, Gower.
18. Jacques, Francois M. (2007), "Even Commodities Have Customers," *Harvard Business Review*, May, 12p.
19. Reichheld, Fred (2006), *The Ultimate Question*, Harvard Business Press, 1st edition, March, 210p.
20. Friedman, Thomas L. (2005), *The World Is Flat*, Farrar, Strauss and Giroux, 1st edition; 2nd updated and expanded edition published in 2006; and now *The World Is Flat 3.0*, Picador, published in 2007.
21. McKinsey & Company (2006), *Profiting from Proliferation,* Allen P. Webb Editor, 131 p.
22. *BusinessWeek* (2008), "The Biggest Bang for the Buck," September 22.
23. Kumar, Nirmalya (2004), *Marketing As Strategy: Understanding the CEO's Agenda for Driving Growth and Innovation*, Harvard Business Press, May, 1st edition, 304p.
24. Young, Roy A., Allen M. Weiss, and Davis W. Steward (2006), *Marketing Champions,* Wiley, September, 1st edition, 288p.

1 The Tide of Commoditization

1. Schrage, Michael (2007), "The Myth of Commoditization," *MIT Sloan Management Review,* Winter, 5p.
2. *Chartic* (2008), "Avoiding the Black Hole of Commoditization," Boston, 4p, www.chartic.com,
3. Shell, Ellen R. (2009), *Cheap,* The Penguin Press, 296p.
4. McKenna, Regis (2002), *Total Access: Giving Customers What They Want in an Anytime, Anywhere World*, Harvard Business Press, March, 1st edition, 250p.
5. Arnst, Catherine (2010), "Radical Surgery," *Bloomberg BusinessWeek,* January 18, 7p.
6. Rogers, Everett M. and Everett Rogers (2003), *Diffusion of Innovations*, Free Press, 5th edition, 512p.
7. Moore, Geoffrey A. (2002), *Crossing the Chasm*, Harper Paperbacks, revised edition, 256p.
8. Larreche, J.C. (2008), *The Momentum Effect: How to Ignite Exceptional Growth,* Wharton School Publishing, 352p.
9. Ohnsman Allan, Jeff Green, and Kae Inoue (2010), "The Humbling of Toyota," *Bloomberg BusinessWeek*, March 22–29, 4p.

10. *The Economist* (2009), "Toyota Slips Up," December 12, 1p.
11. Bower, Joseph L. and Clayton M. Christensen (1995), "Disruptive Technologies: Catching the Wave," *Harvard Business Review,* January, 13p.
12. Anderson, Chris (2008), "Free: Why $ 0.00 Is the Future of Business," *Wired,* March, 8 p.
13. http://www.slate.com/id/2638 (posted on January 30, 1998).
14. Schlender, Brent (2005), "Inside the Shakeup at Sony," *Fortune,* April 4, 9p.
15. Rose, Charlie (2010), "Why Sony Is About to Snap Back," *Bloomberg BusinessWeek,* January 18, 2p.
16. Greenfeld, Karl Taro (2010), "Howard Stringer's Vision," *Harvard Business Review,* April, 5p.
17. McKenna, Regis (2002), *Total Access,* Harvard Business School Press, 252p.
18. Manno, Jack P. (1999), *Privileged Goods: Commoditization and Its Impact on Environment and Society,* Ecological Economics Series, ISEE, Lewis Publishers, 267p.
19. Sirkin, Han, Jim Hemerling, and Arindam Bhattacharya (2008), *Globality: Competing with Everyone from Everywhere for Everything,* Business Plus, 1st edition, 304p.
20. *The Economist* (2007), "When Everything Connects," A Special Report, April, 14p.
21. *Time* (2007), "You: Yes You. You Control the Information Age," December–January, 11p.
22. Cook, Scott (2008), "The Contribution Revolution," *Harvard Business Review,* October, 10p.
23. *Economist.com* (2007), "Social Graph-it," October 18, 2p.
24. Li, Charlene and Josh Bernoff (2008), *Groundswell: Winning in a World Transformed by Social Technologies,* 1st edition, Harvard Business Press, April, 224p.
25. Hove, Jeff (2008), *Crowdsourcing: Why the Power of the Crowd is Driving the Future of Business,* Three Rivers Press, September, 1st edition, 336p.
26. Tapscott, Don and Anthony D. Williams (2008), *Wikinomics: How Mass Collaboration Changes Everything,* Portfolio, Penguin Group, April, expanded edition, 368p.

2 New Markets, New Behaviors: A Global Shift

1. Quelch, John A. and Katherine E. Jocz (2009), "How to Market in a Downturn," *Harvard Business Review,* April, 11p.
2. MacMillan and Larry Selden (2008), "Change with Your Customers—and Win Big," *Harvard Business Review,* December, 1p.
3. Flatters, Paul and Michael Willmott (2009), "Understanding the Post-Recession Consumer," *Harvard Business Review,* July–August, 8p.
4. Beinhocher Eric, Ian Davis, and Lenny Mendonca (2009). "The 10 Trends You Have to Watch," *Harvard Business Review,* July–August, 6p.
5. *The Economist* (2009), "From Buy, Buy, to Bye-Bye," April 4, 1p.
6. Mandel, Michael (2007), "The Consumer Crunch," *BusinessWeek,* November, 4p.
7. Wells, Jennifer (2009), "The Calculating Consumer," *The Globe and Mail,* Friday, April 24, 1p.

8. Knudsen, Trond Riiber, Andreas Randel, and Jorgen Rugholm (2005), "The Vanishing Middle Market," *The McKinsey Quarterly*, November, 3p.
9. Bianco, Anthony (2004), "The Vanishing Mass Market," *BusinessWeek*, July 12, 8p.
10. Court, David and Laxman Narasimhan (2010), "Capturing the World's Emerging Middle Class," *The McKinsey Quarterly*, July, 6p.
11. Grossman, Levy (2006), "*Time's* Person of the Year: You!" *Time*, December 13, 1p.
12. Silverstein Michael J. and Neil Fiske (2003), "Luxury for the Masses," *Harvard Business Review*, April, 10p.
13. Thomas, Dana (2007), *Deluxe: How Luxury Lost Its Luster*, Penguin Books, July, reprint edition, 384p.
14. Silverstein, Michael and Neil Fiske with John Butman (2008), *Trading Up: Why Consumers Want New Luxury Goods and How Companies Do Create Them*, Penguin Group (USA), 320p.
15. *Wired* (2005), "Luxury for All," January, 2p.
16. Esfahani, Elizabeth (2006), "High Class, Low Price," *Business 2.0*, November, 2p.
17. McCall, Bruce (2006), "The New Wal-Mart," *BusinessWeek*, August, 1p.
18. *BusinessWeek* (2007), "Pricey Jeans Are So Passe," July 23, 1p.
19. Fernando, R. and Purkayastha D. (2008), "Body Shop Brand Repositioning to Target the Masstige Segment and Impact of Its Acquisition by L'Oréal," *Case Study*, ICFAI Center for Management Research, 24p.
20. Dolan, Robert J. (1997), "L'Oréal of Paris: Bringing Class to Mass with Plenitude," *Case Study*, Harvard Business Publishing, 37p.
21. Jana, Reena (2008), "Ducking the Price War, Target Highlights Fashion," *BusinessWeek*, October 1, 1p.
22. Gogoi, Pallavi (2008), "The Death of Mass Luxury," *BusinessWeek*, January 17, 1p.
23. Duval, Jean-Baptiste (2009), "Les hypers tirent leur rayon textile à quatre épingles," *LSA*., April 30, No 2088, 2p.
24. Porter, Jane (2008), "Bargain Bin Luxe Online," *BusinessWeek*, November 3, 1p.
25. Woyke, Elizabeth (2006), "Luring Luxury Brands to the Web," *BusinessWeek*, September 25, 1p.
26. Frank, Robert J., Jeffrey P. George, and Laxman Narasimhan (2004), "When Your Competitor Delivers More for Less," *The McKinsey Quarterly*, February, 8p.
27. Aubril, Sylvain (2007), "Le pouvoir d'achat version Leclerc," *LSA*, May 17, No 1998, 1p.
28. *The Economist* (2009), "Burgeoning Burgeoisie: A Special Report on the New Middle Classes in Emerging Markets," February 14, 14p.
29. Farrell, Diana, Ulrich A. Gersch, and Elizabeth Stephenson (2006), "The Value of China's Emerging Middle Class," *The McKinsey Quarterly*, June, special edition, 69p.
30. St-Maurice, Ian, Claudia Sussmuth-Dyckerhoff, and Hsinhsin Tsai (2008), "What's New with the Chinese Consumer," *The McKinsey Quarterly*, October, 10p.
31. Magni, Max and Yuval Atsmon (2010), "A Better Approach to China's Markets," *Harvard Business Review*, March, 3p.
32. Beinhocker, Eric D., Diana Farrell, and Adil S. Zainulbhai (2007), "Tracking the Growth of India's Middle Class," *The McKinsey Quarterly*, August, 11p.

33. Lee, John (2010), "Don't Underestimate India's Consumers," *Bloomberg BusinessWeek*, February 1 & 8, 1p.
34. Elstrodt, Heinz-Peter, Jorge A. Fergie, and Martha A. Laboissiere (2006), "How Brazil Can Grow," *The McKinsey Quarterly*, December, 4p.
35. Gadiesh, Orit, Philip Leung, and Till Vestring (2007), "Battle for China's Good-Enough Market," *Harvard Business Review*, September, 13p.
36. Lecler, Morgan (2008), "Les marques milliardaires, armes anticrise," *LSA*, Novembre, No 2067, 3p.
37. Wileman, Andrew and Michael Jary (1997), *Retail Power Plays: From Trading to Brand Leadership*, NYU Press, August, 280p.
38. Winters, Arthur A., Peggy Fincher Winters, and Carol Paul (2006), *The Power of Retail Branding: Reinvention Strategies for Empowering the Brand*, Visual Reference Publications, 176p.
39. Kumar, Nirmalya, Jan-Benedict, and E.M. Steenkamp (2007), *Private Label Strategy: How to Meet the Store Brand Challenge*, Harvard Business School Press Book, 356p.
40. Boyle, Matthew (2008),"Generics: Making Gains in the Shelf War," *BusinessWeek*, November, 1p.
41. *The Economist* (2008), "The Germans Are Coming," August 16, 1p.
42. Breton, Philippe (2009), "Les nouveaux enjeux des marques de distributeurs," *Décisions Marketing*, January–March, 4p.
43. Yvernault, Veronique (2008), "Les francais se méfient toujours plus des marques," *LSA*, December, No 2071, 2p.
44. Picard, Magaly (2007), "Les fans de MDD, toujours plus jeunes et plus fidèles," *LSA*, May, No 1999, 2p.
45. Aubril, Sylvain (2008), "Les négociations commerciales s'annoncent très dures," *LSA*, October, No 2060, 4p.
46. Monroe, Sarah, David Sinclair, and Tobias A. Wachinger (2009), "Understanding Online Shoppers in Europe," *The McKinsey Quarterly*, May, 4p.
47. Shirky, Clay (2008), *Here Comes Everybody*, The Penguin Press, 328p.
48. McGregor, Jena (2008), "Consumer Vigilantes," *BusinessWeek*, February 21, 4p.
49. Lee, Louise (2005), "Dell: In the Bloghouse," *BusinessWeek*, August 25, 1p.
50. Javis, Jeff (2007), "Dell Learns to Listen," *BusinessWeek*, October 17, 2p.
51. Eisenberg, Bryan and Jeffrey, with Lisa T. Davis, *Waiting for Your Cat to Bark?* Nelson Business, 225p.
52. Walker, Rob (2008), *Buying In*, Random House, 291p.
53. Antinori, Albiera and Lodovico Antinori (2004), *Mondovino*, DVD, Velocity/Thinkfil.

3 The Value-for-Money Business Perspective

1. Riboud, Franck (2009), "La crise impose de repenser le rôle de l'entreprise," *Le Monde*, March 2. 1p (one article).
2. Beinhocker, Eric, Ian Davis, and Lenny Mendonca (2009), "The 10 Trends You Have to Watch," *Harvard Business Review*, July–August, 6p.

3. Haque Humair (2009), "Why Ideals are the New Business Models," Blog, *Harvard Business Publishing*, posted on March 13 (followed by a lot of comments).
4. Heskett, James L., W. Earl Sasser, Jr., and Leonard A. Schlesinger (2003), *The Value Profit Chain: Treat Employees Like Customers and Customers Like Employees*, Free Press, December, 400p.
5. Rappaport, Alfred (2006), "10 Ways to Create Shareholder Value," *Harvard Business Review*, September, 12p.
6. Carrott, Gregory T., Stuart E. Jackson (2009), "Shareholder Value Must Top the CEO's Agenda," *Harvard Business Review*, January, 4p.
7. Moore, Geoffrey A. (2002), *Living on the Fault Line*, Harper Business, revised edition, 277p.
8. Viguerie, Patrick, Sven Smit, and Mehrdad Bachai (2008), *The Granularity of Growth: How to Identify the Sources of Growth and Drive Enduring Company Performance*, Wiley, March, 240p.
9. Rose, Frank (2002), "The Father of Creative Destruction," *Wired*, March, 1p.
10. Foster, Richard and Sarah Kaplan (2001), *Creative Destruction*, Broadway Business, April, 1st edition, 384p.
11. Woodruff, Robert B. (1997), "Customer Value: The Next Source for Competitive Advantage," *Journal of the Academy of Marketing Science*, Vol. 25, No 2, March, 15p.
12. Anderson, James C., James A. Narus, and Wouter van Rossum (2006), "Customer Value Propositions in Business Markets," *Harvard Business Review*, March, 12p.
13. Reichheld, et al. (2007), "Stay Focused on Your Customers—As You Grow Your Business," *Harvard Business Review Newsstand Special Issue*, August, 128p.
14. Anderson, James, James A. Narus (1998), "Business Marketing: Understand What Customers Value," *Harvard Business Review*, November, 11p.
15. http://www.fatwallet.com/forums/finance/526847 (posted on October 2, 2005).
16. Ledingham, Dianne and Darrell K. Rigby (2004), "CRM Done Right," *Harvard Business Review*, November, 11p.
17. Christensen, Clayton M. and Michael E. Raynor (2003), *The Innovator's Solution: Creating and Sustaining Sucessful Growth*, Harvard Business Press, April, 304p.
18. Reena, Jana (2008), "Innovation: The Biggest Bang for the Buck," *BusinessWeek*, September 22, BusinessWeek Innovation Index, 6p (posted on the Web).
19. Quality Research International, permanent glossary, www.qualityresearchinternational.com
20. Williamson, Peter and Ming Zeng (2009), "Value-for-Money Strategies for Recessionary Times," *Harvard Business Review*, March, 11p.
21. Levitt, Theodore (2004), "Marketing Myopia," *Harvard Business Review*, HBR Classic, July, 16p.
22. Braff, Adam and John C. DeVine (2008), "Maintaining the Customer Experience," *The McKinsey Quarterly*, December, 3p.
23. Martin, Roger (2010), "The Age of Customer Capitalism," *Harvard Business Review*, January–February, 8p.
24. Heskett, Sasser, Jr., and Schlesinger (2003)., *The Value Profit Chain*, 400p.

25. Caussil, Jean-Noël (2009), "Le hard discount plus assez puriste?" *LSA,* April, 3p.
26. Porter, Michael (1998), *The Competitive Advantage: Creating and Sustaining Superior Performance,* Free Press, June, 592p.
27. Highly provocative speech on "Moral" Capitalism, given at Davos in 2009.
28. Sanford, Linda S. (2005), *Let Go To Grow: Escaping the Commodity Trap,* Prentice Hall, December, 202p.
29. Berry, Leonard (2007), "The Best Companies Are Generous," *Business Horizons,* July, 7p.
30. McGovern, Gail and Yougme Moon (2007), "Companies and the Customers Who Hate Them," *Harvard Business Review,* June, 7p.

4 Re-Reinventing Business Models

1. Byrne, David (2008), "The Fall and Rise of Music," *Wired,* January, 5p.
2. Hagel III, John, John Seely Brown, and Lang Davison (2008), "Shaping Strategy in a World of Constant Disruption," *Harvard Business Review,* October, 9p.
3. Porter, Michael (1998), *Competitive Advantage,* The Free Press, 1st edition, 592p.
4. Tennent, John (2005), *Guide to Business Modelling,* Bloomberg Press, 2nd edition, 281p.
5. Mc Knight, Thomas K. (2003), *Will It Fly? How to Know if Your New Business Idea Has Wings... Before You Take the Leap,* Financial Times Press, September, 368p.
6. Entrepreneur Press and Don Debelak (2006), *Business Models Made Easy,* Entrepreneur Press, October, 1st edition, 240p.
7. Mitchell, Donald, Carol Coles, B. Thomas Golisano, and Robert B. Knutson (2003), *The Ultimate Competitive Advantage: Secrets of Continually Developing a More Profitable Business Model,* Berrett-Koehler Publishers, 334p.
8. Slywostzky, Andrian J., David J. Morrison, and Bob Andelman (2002), *The Profit Zone: How Strategic Business Design Will Lead You to Tomorrow's Profits,* Three Rivers Press, February, 352p.
9. Peter, Thomas and Robert H. Waterman (1982 and 2004), *In Search of Excellence,* Harper and Row,1st edition; Collins Business, 2nd edition, 400p.
10. Travis, Tom (2007), *Doing Business Anywhere: The Essential Guide to Going Global,* Wiley, April, 202p.
11. Weill, Peter and Michael R. Vitale (2001), *Place to Space: Migrating to Ebusiness Models,* Harvard Business Press, June, 372p.
12. Hax, Arnoldo C., Dean L. Wilde II, and Dr. Lester Thurow (2001), *The delat Project: Discovering New Sources of Profitability in a Networked Economy,* Palgrave Macmillan, 288p.
13. Chesbrough, Henry (2006), *Open Business Models: How to Thrive in the New Innovation,* Harvard Business Press, December, 1st edition, 256p.
14. Berry, Leonard L. (1999), *Discovering the Soul of Service: The Nine Drivers of Sustainable Business Success,* Free Press, February, 268p.

15. Zeithaml, Valerie (1990), *Delivering Quality Service: Balancing Customer Perceptions and Expectations,* Free Press, March, 226p.
16. Heskett, James L., W. Earl Sasser, Jr., and Leonard A. Schlesinger (1997), *The Service Profit Chain,* Free Press, 301p.
17. Reichheld, Frederik F. (1996), *The Loyalty Effect: The Hidden Force Behind Growth, Profits and Lasting Value,* Harvard Business Press, September, 323p.
18. Plaster, Gary and Jerry Alderman (2006), *Beyond Six Sigma: Profitable Growth through Customer Value Creation,* John Wiley, March, 320p.
19. Ibid.
20. ASQ (2005), *ACSI 10-Year Report Analysis (1994–2004),* National Quality Resource Center at the University of Michigan, 108p.
21. Kirsner, Scott (2008), *Inventing the Movies*, CinemaTech Books, 213p.
22. *Knowledge@Wharton* (2008), "Inventing the Movies: The Epic Battle between Innovation and the Status Quo in Hollywood"(posted on the Web on August 20), 3p.
23. *The Economist* (2008), "Coming Soon," Briefing, Hollywood and the Internet, February, 4p.
24. *Fortune* (2007), "The Mytunes Revolution," August, 5p.
25. Levine, Robert (2007), "You Ought to be In Pictures," *Business 2.0,* April, 7p.
26. Quittner, Josh (2010). "The Future of Reading," *Fortune*, March 1, 8p.
27. *The Economist* (2008), "Telemedecine Comes Home," The Economist Technology Quarterly, June, 3p.
28. Roth, Daniel (2010), "The Future of Money," *Wired,* March, 10p.
29. Lehman-Orthega Laurence and Jean-marc Schoetti (2005), "From Buzzword to Managerial Tool: The Role of Business Models in Strategic Innovation," Article presented at CLADEA, Santiago de Chile, 14p (posted on the Web).
30. Breen, Bill and Gary Hamel (2007), *The Future of Management*, Harvard Business Press, September, 1st edition, 288p.
31. Afuah, Allan (2009), *Strategic Innovation: New Game Strategies for Competitive Advantage*, Routledge, 1st edition, 484p.
32. Hamel, Gary and C. K. Prahalad (1996), *Competing for the Future,* Harvard Business Press, April, 357p.
33. Timmers, Peter (1998), "Business Models for Electronic Commerce," *Electronic Markets*, Vol. 8, No 2, 6p.
34. Lehman-Orthega Laurence and Jean-marc Schoetti (2005), "From Buzzword to Managerial Tool: The Role of Business Models in Strategic Innovation, " Article presented at CLADEA, Santiago de Chile, 14p (posted on the Web).
35. Shafer, S. M., Smith, H. J., and Linder, J. C. (2005), "The Power of Business Models," *Business Horizons,* Vol 48, No 3, 9p.
36. Rappa, M. (2003), *Managing the Digital Enterprise,* posted at, http://digitalenterprise.org/
37. Ple, Loic, Lecoq Xavier, and Jacques Angot (2009), "Customer-integrated Business Models: A Theoretical Framework," posted on the Web, LEM, 49p, http://lem.cnrs.fr/Portals/2/actus/DP_200824.pdf
38. Plaster, Gary and Jerry Alderman (2006), *Beyond Six Sigma: Profitable Growth through Customer Value Creation,* John Wiley, March, 320p.

39. Johnson, Mark W., Clayton M. Christensen, and Henning Kagermann (2008), "Reinventing Your Business Model," *Harvard Business Review*, December, 9p.
40. Plaster and Alderman (2006), *Beyond Six Sigma,* 320p.
41. Ibid.
42. Osterwalder, Alex (2005), "Zara Business Model," *Web Site on Business Model Design and Integration*, June, 1p.
43. Duval, Jean-Baptiste (2008), "Plongee dans les coulisses de Zara," *LSA*, December, No. 2070, 6p.
44. Vijay Govindarajan and Chris Trimble (2005), "Building Breakthrough Business Within Established Organizations," *Harvard Business Review*, May, 10p.
45. Loren, Gary (2004), "Dow Corning's Push for Organic Growth," *Strategy and Innovation Article,* Harvard Business Publishing, November, 3p.
46. Kashari, K. and Francis, I. (2006), "Xiameter: The Past and Future of a Disruptive Innovation," *Case*, IMD, 21p.

5 An Integrated Set of New Business Logics

1. Krugman, Paul and Sarah Cliffe (2009), "Economist Paul Krugman on being surprised by the spread of the downturn," *Harvard Business Review,* June, 2p.
2. Argawal, Anupal, Eric Harmon, and Michael Viertler (2009), "Cutting Sales Costs, Not Revenues," *The McKinsey Quarterly*, March, 10p.
3. Bettencourt, Lance A., and Anthony W. Ulwick (2008), "The Customer-Centered Innovation Map," *Harvard Business Review*, May, 6p.
4. Doyle, Peter (2000), *Value-Based Marketing for Corporate Growth and Shareholder Value,* Wiley, 1st edition, 384p.
5. Royston, Mary (2006), *What is Values-Based Marketing,* posted on the Web, Credit Unions Com, 1p.
6. DeBonis, Nicholas J., Eric W. Balinski, and Philipp Allen (2002), *Value-Based Marketing for Bottom-Line Success,* McGraw-Hill, 288p.
7. Kumar, Nirmalya (2004), *Marketing As Strategy; Understanding the CEO's Agenda for Driving Growth and Innovation*, Harvard Business Press, May, 1st edition, 304p.
8. Shiffman, Denise (2008), *The Age of Engage,* Hunt Street Press, 220p.
9. Tapscott, Don (2008), *Wikinomics*, Portfolio Hardcover, expanded edition, 368p.
10. Surowiecki, James (2005), *The Wisdom of Crowds*, Anchor, August, 336p.
11. Howe, Jeff (2008), *Crowdsourcing: Why the Power of the Crowd Is Driving the Future of Business*, The Three Rivers Press, September, 336p.
12. Tapscott, Don (2008), *Grown Up Digital*, McGraw-Hill, October, 1st edition, 384p.
13. Godin, Seth (1999), *Permission Marketing*, Simon and Schuster, 1st edition, 256p.
14. Godin, Seth (2008), *Tribes: We Need You to Lead Us*, Portfolio Hardcover, 1st edition, 160p.
15. Jaffe, Joseph (2007), *Join the Conversation*, Wiley, October, 320p.
16. McGregor, Jena (2009), "The Hard Sell," *BusinessWeek,* October 15, 2p.
17. Lloyd, Tracey (2010), "How a Decade of War Has Created a New Generation of Elite Business Leaders," *Fortune,* March 22, 10p.

18. Li, Charlene (2008), *Groundswell: Winning in a World Transformed by Social Technologies*, Harvard Business Press, April, 1st edition, 224p.
19. Scott, David Erman (2009), *The New Rules of Marketing & PR*, Wiley, 2nd edition, 287p.
20. Baker, Stephen (2009), "What's a Friend Worth?" *BusinessWeek,* June 1, 3p.
21. *BusinessWeek* (2009), "Managing the Tweets," June 1, 2p.
22. Stull, Craig, Phill Myers, and David Meerman Scott (2008), *Tuned In*, Wiley, June, 1st edition, 224p.
23. Braff, Adam and John C. Devine (2008), "Maintaining the Customer Experience," *The McKinsey Quarterly*, December, 4p.
24. Lenskold, James D. (2003), *Marketing ROI: The Path to Campaign, Customer and Corporate Profitability,* McGraw-Hill, July, 1st edition, 256p.
25. Davis, John (2006), *Measuring Marketing; 103 Key Metrics Every Marketer Needs,* Wiley, November, 1st edition, 440p.
26. McKinsey (2009), "Measuring Marketing: McKinsey Global Survey Results," *The McKinsey Quarterly,* March, 9p.
27. Peppers, Don and Martha Rogers (2005), *Return on Customer: Creating Maximum Value From Your Scarcest Resource*, Broadway Business, June, 304p.
28. Anderson, James C. and James A. Narus (1998), "Business Marketing: Understand What Customers Value," *Harvard Business Review,* November, 11p.
29. Gouillart, Francis J. and Frederick D. Sturdivant (1994), "Spend a Day in the Life of Your Customers," *Harvard Business Review,* January, 10p.
30. Anderson, James C., James A. Narus, and Wouter Van Rossum (2006), "Customer Value Propositions in Business Models," *Harvard Business Review,* March, 12p.
31. Jana, Reena (2009), "Inspiration from Emerging Economies," *BusinessWeek,* March 23 & 30, 3p.
32. Immelt, Jeffrey R., Vijay Govindarajan, and Chris Trimble (2009), "How GE Is Disrupting Itself," *Harvard Business Review,* September, 12p.
33. Kao, John (2009), "Tapping the World's Innovation Hot Spots," *Harvard Business Review,* March, 9p.
34. McKinsey (2007), "How Companies Approach Innovation," *The McKinsey Quarterly*, October, 13p.
35. Selden, Larry and Ian C. MacMillan (2006), "Manage Customer-Centric Innovation Systematically," *Harvard Business Review,* April, 9p.
36. Coyne, Kevin P. and Patricia Gorman Clifford (2007), "Breakthrough Thinking from Inside the Box," *Harvard Business Review,* December, 8p.
37. *Harvard Business Review* (2009), "Rebuilding Trust," Introduction to a Spotlight on Trust, June, p. 53.
38. O'Toole, James and Warren Bennis (2009), "A Culture of Candor," *Harvard Business Review,* June, 9p.
39. Podolny, Joel M. (2009), "The Buck Stops (and Starts) at Business School," *Harvard Business Review,* June, 6p.
40. Kelly, Kevin (2009), "The New Socialism," *Wired,* June, 6p.
41. Gates, Bill (2005), interview on CNET news.com, January.

42. Kramer, Roderick M. (2009), "Rethinking Trust," *Harvard Business Review*, June, 9p.
43. Vargo, Stephen and Robert Lusch (2004), "Evolving to a New Dominant Logic for Marketing," *Journal of Marketing*, January, Vol 68, 17p.
44. Lusch, Robert F. and Stepen L. Vargo (2006), *The Service-dominant Logic of Marketing: Dialog, Debate, and Directions,* M.E. Sharpe, 449p.
45. Read, Stuart, Nicholas Dew, Saras D. Sarasvathy, Michael Song, and Robert Wilbank (2009), "Marketing Under Uncertainty: The Logic of an Effectual Approach," *Journal of Marketing*, January, Vol 68, 17p.
46. Sarasvathy, Saras D. (2009), *Effectuation: Elements of Entrepreneurial Expertise,* Edward Elgar Pub, May, 368p.

6 CVC Approaches: The Disruption Spectrum

1. Johnson, William C. and Art Weinstein (2004), *Superior Customer Value in the New Economy*, CRC Press, 2nd edition, 434p.
2. Poudstone, William (2010), *Priceless: The Myth of Fair Value (and How to Take Advantage of It)*, Hill and Wang, January, 336p.
3. Reilly, Tom (2010), *Crush Price Objections: Sales Tactics for Holding Your Ground and Protecting Your Profit*, McGraw-Hill, January, 1st edition, 182p.
4. ACSI, www.theacsi.org.
5. Hanssens, Dominique M., Daniel Thorpe, and Carl Finkbeiner (2008), "Marketing When Customer Equity Matters," *Harvard Business Review*, May, 7p.
6. Nunes, Paul F., Woodruff W. Driggs, David Herman, Jeffrey F. Rayport, Stephen Dull, and Joe Scaffido (2006), "What Serves Customer Best?" *HBR Case Study and Commentary*, October, 10p.
7. Varadajan, Rajan (2009), "Fortune at the Bottom of the Innovation Pyramid: The Strategic Logic of Incremental Innovation," *Business Horizons*, 52, 9p.
8. Ansoff, Igor (1957), "Strategies for Diversification," *Harvard Business Review*, September–October, 12p.
9. Bhargava, Rohit (2008), *Personality Not Included: Why Companies Lose Their Authenticity And How Great Brands Get if Back*, McGraw-Hill, May, 1st edition, 300p.
10. Einsigerich, Andreas B., Gunyan Bhadivaj, and Yoshio Miyamoto (2010), "Behold the Extremes Consumers..." *Harvard Business Review*, April, 2p.
11. Levy, Steven (2009), "All Grown Up," *Wired*, January, 5p.
12. Helm, Burt (2009), "Bowing Up Pepsi," *BusinessWeek*, April 27, 5p.
13. Farzad, Roben (2009), "Merill's Bleeding Brand," *BusinessWeek*, March 9, 1p.
14. McGregor, Jean (2009), "When Service Means Survival," *BusinessWeek*, March 2, 7p.
15. Shankar, Venkatesh, Leonard L. Berry, and Thomas Dotzel (2009), "A Practical Guide to Combining Product Plus Services," *Harvard Business Review*, November, 6p.
16. Auguste, Byron G., Eric P. Harmon, and Vivek Pandit (2006), "The Right Service Strategies for Product Companies," *The McKinsey Quarterly*, No 1, 11p.

17. Lusch, Robert F. and Stephen L. Vargo (2006), *The Service-dominant Logic of Marketing:Dialog, Debate And Directions,* M.E. Sharpe, February, 449p.
18. Heskett, James L., W. Earl Sasser, and Leonard A. Schlesinger (1997), *The Service Profit Chain,* Free Press, April, 320p.
19. MacMillan, Ian C. and Larry Selden (2008), "The Incumbent's Advantage," *Harvard Business Review*, October, 9p.
20. Anderson, Chris (2008), "The PetaByte Age: The End of Theory," *Wired*, June, 2p.
21. Alexander, Whit and Dorian Stone (2009), "How US Consumer Spending Is Changing," *The McKinsey Quarterly*, June, 4p.
22. Welch, David (2009), "The Incredible Shrinking Boomer Economy," *BusinessWeek*, August 3, 4p.
23. Bohlen, Betsy, Steve Carlotti, and Liz Mihas (2009), "How the Recession Has Changed US Consumer Behavior," *The McKinsey Quarterly*, December, 4p.
24. *Knowledge@Wharton* (2007), "Brand Managers' High-wire Act: Going Global and Staying Local," October 31, 4p.
25. Lay, Philip, Todd Hewlin, and Geoffrey Moore (2009), "In a Downturn, Provoke Your Customers," *Harvard Business Review*, March, 9p.
26. Caillace, Laure (2008), "Le magasin de demain, c'est déjà aujourd'hui", *LSA*, February 14, 4p.
27. Favaro, Ken, Tim Romberger, and David Meer (2009), "Five Rules for Retailing in a Recession," *Harvard Business Review*, April, 8p.
28. Hemp, Paul (2006), "Are You Ready for E-tailing 2.0?" *Harvard Business Review*," October, 3p.
29. Anderson, Chris (2006), *The Long Tail*, Hyperion, 256p.
30. Brybjolfsson, Erik, Yu Jeffrey Hu, and Michael D. Smith (2006), "From Niches to Riches: Anatomy of the Long Tail," *MIT/Sloan Management Review*, Summer, 5p.
31. Elberse, Anita (2008), "Should You Invest in the Long Tail?" *Harvard Business Review,* July–August, 8p.
32. Quelch, John (2008), "Long-Tail Economics? Give Me Blockbusters!" *Harvard Working Knowledge*, September 10, 3p.
33. Joyce, John (2009), "*Pandora and the Music Project,"* Scientific Computing, www.scientificcomputing.com.
34. Capell, Kerry (2009), "Novartis Radically Remaking Its Drug Business," *BusinessWeek*, June 22, 5p.
35. McGregor, Jena (2008), "At Best Buy, Marketing Goes Micro," *BusinessWeek*, May 26, 1p.
36. Brown, Tim (Interview) (2009), "Lessons from Innovation's Front Lines: An Interview with IDEO's CEO," *The McKinsey Quarterly*, November, 7p.
37. Capps, Robert (2009), "Why Lo-fi High Tech Will Rule the World," *Wired*, September, 9p.
38. Solis, Brian (2007), "Five Characteristics of Marketing 2.0—And Why You Should Care," *Social Computing Magazine*, July10, 2p, www.socialcomputingmagazine.com.
39. Fournier, Susan and Lara Lee (2009), "Getting Brand Communities Right," *Harvard Business Review*, April, 7p.

40. Merholz, Peter (2009), "How to Extend Your Customer Experience Through Social Media," *Blog Post from Harvardbusiness.org*, August 24, 2p.
41. Hof, Robert D. (2009), "Betting on the Real-Time Web," *BusinessWeek*, August 17, 4p.
42. *The Economist* (2009), "Tweeting All the Way to the Bank," July 25, 2p.
43. Tapscott, Don (2008), *Wikinomics*, Portfolio Hardcover, expanded edition, 368p.
44. Koerner, Brendan I. (2006), "Geeks in Toyland," *Wired*, February, 8p.
45. Robertson, David and Per Hjuler (2009), "Innovating: A Turnaround at Lego," *Wired*, September, 2p.
46. Huston, Larry and Nabbil Sakkab (2006), "Inside Procter & Gamble's New Model for Innovation," *Harvard Business Review*, March, 10p.
47. Edwards, Cliff (2007), "The Road to WiMax," *BusinessWeek*, September 3, 6p.
48. Oram, Andy (2001), *Peer-to-Peer: Harnessing the Power of Disruptive Technologies*, O'Reilly Media, Inc., 448p.
49. Helm, Burt (2006), "BitTorrent Goes Hollywood," *BusinessWeek*, May, 2p.
50. Kim, Chan W; and Renée Mauborgne (2005), *Blue Ocean Strategy: How to Create Uncontested Market Space and Make Competition Irrelevant*, Harvard Business Press, February, 1st edition, 256p.
51. Nidumulo, Ram, C. K. Prahalad, and M. R. Rangaswami (2009), "Why Sustainability Is Now the Key Driver of Innovation," *Harvard Business Review*, September, 8p.

Conclusion

1. Kirby, Julia and Thomas A. Stewart (2007), "The Institutional Yes," *Harvard Business Review*, October, 9p.
2. Cooper, Frank (2009), *The Customer Signs Your Paycheck*, McGraw-Hill, August, 1st edition, 240p.
3. Larréché, Jean-Claude (2008), *The Momentum Effect*, Wharton School Publishing, December, 1st edition, 352p.
4. *The Economist* (2009), "The Other-Worldly Philosophers," July 18, 3p.
5. *The Economist* (2009), "Efficiency and Beyond," July 18, 2p.
6. Ariely, Dan (2009), "The End of Rational Economics," *Harvard Business Review*, July–August, 7p.
7. Davis, Gerald (2009), "The Rise and Fall of Finance and the End of the Society of Organizations," Academy of Management Science, August, 18p.
8. Heracleous, Loizos and Luh Luh Lan (2010), "The Myth of Shareholder Capitalism," *Harvard Business Review*, April, 1p.
9. Clinton, Bill, President (2009), "Creating Value in an Economic Crisis," *Harvard Business Review*, September, 2p.
10. Cohen, Daniel (2009), "Une crise qui ne règle pas les problèmes qui l'ont générée," *Le Monde*, August 31 (posted on www.lemonde.fr).
11. Bruch, Heike and Jochen I. Menges (2010), "The Acceleration Trap," *Harvard Business Review,* April, 7p.

12. Miles, Robert H. (2010), "Accelerating Corporate Transformations (Don't Lose Your Nerve!)", *Harvard Business Review,* January–February, 7p.
13. Gulati, Ranjay (2007),"Silo Busting," *Harvard Business Review*, Spotlight, May, 9p.
14. *The Economist* (2006), "The Physical Internet: A Survey of Logistics," June 17, 14p.
15. Edelman, David C. (2010), "Four Ways to Get More Value from Digital Marketing," *The McKinsey Quarterly,* March, 8p.
16. Hamel, Gary (2009), "Moon Shots for Management," *Harvard Business Review*, February, 8p.
17. Prokesch, Steven (2009), "How GE Teaches Teams to Lead Change," *Harvard Business Review*, January, 8p.
18. Immelt, Jeffrey R., Vijay Govindarajan, and Chris Trimble (2009), "How GE Is Disrupting Itself," *Harvard Business Review,* October, 11p.
19. Kotter, John (2008), *A Sense of Urgency*, Harvard Business Press, September, 1st edition,128p.
20. Collins, Jim (2009), *How the Mighty Fall: And Why Some Companies Never Give In*, Jim Collins, May, 1st edition, 240p.
21. O'Neill, Michael (2005), "A Perpetual Crisis Machine," *Fortune*, September 19, 10p.
22. Kim, Chan W. and Renée Mauborgne (2009), "How Strategy Shapes Structure," *Harvard Business Review*, September, 8p.
23. Pisano, Gary P. and Roberto Verganti (2008), "Which Kind of Collaboration Is Right for You?" *Harvard Business Review*, December, 9p.
24. Reiss, Spencer (2008), "Planet Amazon," *Wired*, May, 5p.
25. Rigby, Darrell K, Kara Gruver, and James Allen (2009), "Innovation in Turbulent Times," *Harvard Business Review*, June, 8p.
26. Ries, Al and Laura Ries (2009), *War in the Boardroom: Why Left-Brain Management and Right-Brain Marketing Don't See Eye-to-Eye and What to Do About It*, Collins Business, February, 1st edition, 304p.
27. Chambers, John (2008), "CISCO Sees the Future," *Harvard Business Review*, Interview, November, 7p.
28. Carey, Dennis, Michael Patsalos-Fox, and Michael Useem (2009), "Leadership Lessons for Hard Times," *The McKinsey Quarterly*, July, 9p.
29. McKinsey&Company (2009), "Leaders in the Crisis", *The McKinsey Quarterly*, August, 10p.
30. Heifetz, Ronald, Alexander Grashow, and Marty Linsky (2009), "Leadership in a (Permanent) Crisis," *Harvard Business Review*, July–August, 8p.
31. Hill, Linda A. and Paul Hemp (2008), "Where Will We Find Tomorrow's Leaders?" A conversation with Linda A. Hill, *Harvard Business Review*, January, 7p.
32. De Smet, Aron, Monica McGurk, and Marc Vinson (2009), "Unlocking the Potential of Frontline Managers," *The McKinsey Quarterly*, August, 9p.
33. Black, Stewart J. and Hal B. Gregersen (2008), *It Starts with One*, Wharton School Publishing, 162p.
34. Pfeffer, Jeffrey (2009), "Shareholders First? Not So Fast..." *Harvard Business Review*, July–August, 3p.
35. Meyer, Christopher and Andre Schwager (2007), "Understanding Customer Experience," *Harvard Business Review*, February, 10p.

36. Braff, Adam and John C. DeVine (2008), "Maintaining the Customer Experience," *The McKinsey Quarterly*, December, 5p.
37. Lafley, A. G. (2009), "What Only the CEO Can Do," *Harvard Business Review*, May, 9 p.
38. D'Aveni, Richard A. (2007), "Mapping Your Competitive Advantage," *Harvard Business Review*, November, 12p.
39. Brandenburger, Adam M. and Barry J. Nalibuff (1997), *Co-Opetition*, Broadway Business, December, 1st edition, 304p.
40. Ibid.

INDEX

Christian Dussart is a full professor in the Department of Marketing at HEC Montréal and Distinguished SMA Professor for the Society of Marketing Advances (SMA). He is also a visiting professor at HEC Paris. He received his Higher Business School Degree and his Master of Arts from the University of Sherbrooke, Québec, Canada and his PhD from the Catholic University of Louvain-la-Neuve, Belgium in 1986. Before joining HEC Montréal, Professor Dussart held academic positions at the University of Sherbrooke, University of Ottawa, Ontario, the University of Québec at Montreal, Paris Graduate School of Management, Solvay Business School, Brussels, Sorbonne, Paris, CEDEP & INSEAD, Fontainebleau, Tuck School of Business, Dartmouth College and MIT, Sloan.

Dussart specializes in the areas of customer value creation, positioning, digital marketing strategy, globalization, and wiki-marketing and is published in both English and French. He is currently researching the reinvention of business models with both an effectual approach and a service-dominant logic of marketing.

His academic accomplishments are accompanied by practical experience in the field. He was the President of La Brioche Dorée, a fast-food chain in Canada and the United States from 1977–1980, the President and Chairman of Dussart Marketing and Research from 1984–1992, and the President and Chairman of Dussart Independent France from 1992–1998. In addition, he served as the President of Sogemark from 1998–2004 and is a member of the board of the AFM (French Marketing Association). He is now acting as President of Digiworld Inc.

As a truly global author, Dussart has written several books in both English and in French and has published near 100 articles in referred reviews, magazines, and proceedings around the world.

He is a renowned speaker in both academic and business conferences.